8/03

open &
distance
learning
series

D1039024

DELIVERING
LEARNING
on the Net

the why, what & how
of online education

martin weller

KOGAN
PAGE

First published in 2002

Kogan Page Limited
120 Pentonville Road
London N1 9NJ
UK

Stylus Publishing Inc.
22883 Quicksilver Drive
Sterling VA 20166–2012
USA

British Library Cataloguing in Publication Data

A CIP record for this book is available from the British Library

ISBN 0 7494 3675 1

Typeset by Jean Cussons Typesetting, Diss, Norfolk
Printed and bound in Great Britain by Biddles Ltd, Guildford and King's Lynn
www.biddles.co.uk

Contents

Foreword

The recent decision by the UK government to increase the participation rate of 18- to 30-year-olds in higher education to 50 per cent by the year 2010 represents a major national challenge and a unique opportunity. In the current financial climate it will simply not be possible to 'scale up' provision, increase staff numbers and fund another 75 universities. We will have to teach in some other way: online learning via the Net offers a means of doing so. Needless to say, this is not a challenge unique to the UK. It is one that both developed and developing countries are facing, and is why this book is so timely.

Whether you are an 'early adopter' or one of the 'late majority' – a teacher, trainer, administrator or decision maker – you will find the arguments persuasive. In particular, I believe you will be convinced that the future of online learning is as a medium for communication, not a delivery method; it will be an online learning environment where pedagogy and technology are interrelated and where interaction is paramount.

The good news is that you do not need to be a 'techie' to read and benefit from *Delivering Learning on the Net*. Martin has succeeded in assembling an extremely informative and thought-provoking book that is deceptively simple in its style - a difficult balance to achieve. The book also complements several existing titles in the Kogan Page 'Open and Distance Learning Series', adding to the significant body of work that they represent. His discussion of the pedagogy provides an invaluable link to *Learning and Teaching in Distance Education* by Otto Peters and to *Flexible Learning in a Digital World* by Betty Collis and Jeff Moonen. His references to the role of facilitators of online learning will introduce you to the world of *E-Moderating* by Gilly Salmon, while the prospect of a virtual university and resource-based learning is extended by Steve Ryan and his co-authors in *The Virtual University*. The insights Martin provides in his description of the highly successful Open University course 'T171 You, Your Computer and the Net' complement the case studies offered by Tom Vincent and Marc Eisenstadt in *The Knowledge Web* and by Fred Lockwood and Anne Gooley in *Innovations in Open and Distance Learning*.

If you are looking for a book that is written in plain English that dispels myths, provides a sound basis for success and offers lessons for implementation, then look no further. I believe that, with this book, Martin has made a significant contribution to the revolution in learning and teaching.

Fred Lockwood

Acknowledgements

There are of course more people to thank in the writing of any one book than can ever be acknowledged. How far back does one go? Trying to isolate the significant influences becomes an arduous and self-defeating task. Should I thank my English teacher, my university lecturers, the authors of the books and articles that have inspired me? One has to know where to stop if this section is not to resemble one of those Oscar ceremony acceptance speeches which one fears may never end. So I will mention those people who have had a direct input to the book, whilst recognizing this is only the tip of the iceberg.

First, I would like to thank my Open University colleague John Naughton, for his encouragement to engage in a number of interesting projects which eventually led me here. A number of other colleagues read drafts of this book and applied their usual integrity and honesty to the feedback. These include Ley Robinson, Ray Corrigan (particularly for his help with intellectual property issues), Ernie Taylor, Nick Heap (for being concerned about my academic credibility), Clem Herman and Nick Meara. Will Reader also helped me clarify some of my ideas and opinions through our enjoyable e-mail conversations.

Much of the experience this book draws from was gained through chairing an Open University course, T171: You, Your Computer and the Net. I would like to thank all the members of the course team who have worked so hard to make it a success and also the tutors and students of the course, who have created such a rich community. The support of colleagues in the Faculty of Technology, and particularly in the Department of Telematics, where I have explored a number of the ideas in this book through (sometimes shambolic) presentations, is also gratefully acknowledged.

In the publication of this book Fred Lockwood provided excellent advice at the proposal stage and my editor Jonathan Simpson was both tolerant and understanding.

Lastly, I would like to thank my wife Sarah, who listened patiently to my more fanciful ideas and then calmly dissuaded me from them. While I pretended this writing business was difficult, she quietly got on with the real work of carrying and then looking after our first child, Ellen.

For Sarah

Introduction

Who this book is for

Over the past few years I have been involved with a number of online courses, or Net based aspects of distance education courses. I have also written a number of journal and conference papers about these experiences. It was while attending these conferences that the idea for this book began to grow. While there was a good deal of theory in publication, and a lot of experiential papers, the point of these conferences seemed to be the practical discussions that arose over lunch and drinks: the exchange of real experience, problems and opinions. This was an area where feelings often ran high, because the use of the Net in education actually made people address far deeper issues regarding the value of education and the best ways of practising it. For many educators who had previously only lectured face to face, this was the first time they were facing such concerns. The demands of students who may be spatially and temporally distant from them forced them to engage with issues they had previously taken for granted. For others, who were experienced at distance learning, the move to online provision raised a new set of problems. It was these matters we would discuss in detail, swapping ideas, anecdotes and views.

While there were some very good books focusing on specific elements of the online education area, I felt there were relatively few which gave a global, yet personal view. This is what I set out to do in this book, to distil much of the current thinking, practice and debate and place this within an accessible framework.

Why should this be worth doing? My feeling is that the primary responsibility of educators is to be knowledgeable in their own fields. Maintaining this knowledge is, in itself, a difficult task. If a shift to online education also demands expertise in pedagogy and Internet technologies, as well as a deep understanding of wider educational issues and models of successful online operation, then it becomes an arduous, if not impossible, task for an educator. As José Saramago once wrote, 'A man must read widely, a little of everything or whatever he can, but given the shortness of life and the verbosity of the world, not too much should be demanded of him.' Much the same might be said of educators: given the need to stay current in their own field, they cannot realistically be expected to go far beyond this. And while the Net has eased the access to information, it has also greatly increased the 'verbosity of the world'. In order to successfully implement online education I do not feel it is necessary for everyone to read papers relating to all aspects while simultaneously becoming expert developers with a range of software. Given the diversity of circumstances in which any one educator operates it would be foolhardy to prescribe a formula for success. Rather, a broad overview which raises the main issues is probably a sufficient platform from which most educators can develop and refine their own experience and opinions.

One potential audience for this book is the educator who is keen to develop online courses, or is currently delivering an online course and wishes to gain some further insight and is not sure where to start. This book will hopefully provide adequate coverage of all the issues which may be of concern, and if not, then it should help in deciding which areas need further exploration.

Another reader of this book might be the decision maker or administrator in a university who is responsible for online provision. By taking a broad overview of the relevant issues, from assessment to technology and pedagogy to e-commerce, the book will hopefully inform this reader as to potential problems which may arise and also possible solutions.

A third audience might be those working in the commercial sector providing online training or working for private universities. Although much of the discussion is based around university education, the Net brings commercial provision and traditional university education into closer proximity than ever before. This is discussed in detail in Chapter 2 of the book. Many of the issues facing university educators are the same for commercial providers, for the commercial organizations represent the flip-side to the university issue. For instance, the commercialization of education, which is associated with the rise of online provision, is seen as a potential cause for concern among those in higher education, while it is an opportunity for those in the commercial sector. Both parties will feel the consequences of the other's reaction to this change.

Lastly, the book will, I hope, appeal to a general audience who have an interest in the changes occurring in online education. The use of the Net is seen by many as a very significant change in educational practice and structure. If education is at the heart of society, as many people feel it should be, then these changes will affect us all. This audience might include students (those studying education specifically, or those with an interest in the impact of technology), Net enthusiasts and detractors, parents and employers. All will have an interest in how education and, by extension, society are shaped by the use of new technologies, and conversely, how the technologies themselves adapt to the demands of the educational arena.

The contents of the book

This is a book of three parts essentially, and different sections may appeal more or less to the different audiences outlined above. The structure of the book reflects its subtitle, focusing on the why, what and how of online education.

The first four chapters take a broader view of the Net and its relation to education. These chapters represent the 'why' of online education. They explore issues such as why the Net has a greater potential as an educational technology than many of its predecessors, the issues online provision raises for universities, the lessons we can draw from e-commerce, and some of the current motivations for adopting the Net in education. For the educator concerned with practical issues of implementation, these may initially seem rather abstract. I would argue, however, that it is important to form a view as to the role of the Net in education and its potential impact, since this will shape the actual use of it by both individuals and organizations.

The next five chapters are more concerned with the 'what' of online education, by looking at issues relating to the implementation of online courses. These focus on pedagogy, communication, new working methods, assessment and technology. Those who are more interested in the impact of education and policy may feel these chapters are focused on more practical issues. However, the broader issues will be shaped by the decisions made by the practitioners.

Each chapter ends with a section entitled Lessons for Implementation, which attempts to synthesize the discussion of the chapter into useful suggestions for educators. These sections constitute the 'how' of the subtitle, by addressing practical issues of implementation.

If the first four chapters appeal to those with a top-down mentality and the next five to those who prefer a bottom-up approach, then the last two provide a conclusion for both approaches. The penultimate chapter suggests a framework for looking at the issues surrounding online courses. The last chapter pulls several threads together, providing an analogy from a different industry, looking at significant issues over the next few years and a hypothetical course of the future.

While I would encourage every reader to read the whole of the book, given the demands on time I have mentioned above, different audiences may choose to focus on some chapters more than others.

The approach of the book

Given the demands on educators' time to stay knowledgeable in their own field, I felt a sense of duty to make this book as accessible as possible. Reading any academic text outside one's domain of expertise is difficult enough, but an overly dense writing style makes the reading quickly seem a burden, then a chore. Although I hope there are sufficient references, the book also contains accounts of my own experience and a good deal of personal opinion. My feeling is that it is far more engaging to be arguing or agreeing with someone, in essence to be taking part in a discussion (albeit a slightly one-sided one), than simply to be spoken to.

Lastly, the introduction to any such book always contains an excuse for why it exists in this form, and not as a Web site. A fair enough accusation: one often gets the feeling when reading books by Net evangelists that while the Net for everything is the philosophy we should adopt, it does not apply to the author. In my case I have no qualms about this being in a book format. One of the points raised in the book is about the appropriate use of media, and books represent an excellent format for this type of one-to-many information delivery. Although I have suggested that different types of reader may prefer to focus on different parts of the book, it is nonetheless essentially a linear text. Such a text would not particularly benefit from the non-linear, hypermedia aspect of Web delivery. Having said this, there is an accompanying Web site, which contains further references and comments. This can be found at http://kn.open.ac.uk/deliveringlearning.

If there is any chapter or topic in particular that interests you, then I would urge you to use the Web site to find references which will enable you to explore it in further detail. This hybrid approach allows the text in this book to remain relatively uncluttered by an abundance of references, while still providing the detail for those who wish to go deeper in to a subject.

For educators, the Net represents both a terrific challenge and an opportunity. The next five years or so will determine how it is used in education, or, depending on your perspective, how it uses education. I view involvement now as being like buying shares in the early stages of a company like IBM or Microsoft: a small outlay now will reap great rewards later (although not necessarily financial ones). I can think of no more exciting time to be involved in education, and I hope this book helps in some way to clarify issues, or encourage people in that participation.

Chapter 1

Why the Net is significant

Introduction

The way in which any institution, company or individual views the Net will have a significant effect on the manner in which they employ it and the sort of tasks for which they feel it is best suited. In this and the following two chapters I wish to address some of the common views about the Internet in education, and stress why I believe the shift to online delivery represents a significant change in educational practice. You may not agree, but it is important to think about how you view the Net and its role in education before embarking upon issues of online delivery. Nearly all of these issues will flow from this underlying viewpoint, so it is worth making it explicit to yourself and others.

This chapter begins with an account of a large-scale Web course I have worked on, which will be used as an example throughout the book. The promise of educational technology and some of the disappointment surrounding this is then discussed. Many educators rightly approach the Net with a degree of scepticism, thinking they have heard all of these claims before for technologies which are now either obsolete or peripheral. The remainder of this chapter outlines the reasons why we should view the Net as a significant educational technology.

You, your computer and the Net

First, let me start with a brief tale of a course I was heavily involved with. I will return to this throughout the book as a source of examples. The course in question is called 'You, Your Computer and the Net', but it will be referred to by its course code, T171, for simplicity. The course was developed at the United Kingdom Open University (OU). For those who are unfamiliar with the OU, it is a solely distance education university, with over 150,000 students studying part-time annually. Founded in 1969, the OU has developed a distance learning approach based predominantly around the use of specifically authored printed units. Students are allocated to part-time tutors (or Associate Faculty) who offer support through regular face to face tutorials, detailed feedback on assignments, and contact via telephone, e-mail or letter.

In 1997 a group of us at the OU had an idea to create an introductory course on computers and the Internet. Those involved were enthusiastic, some might say evangelical, about the Internet and its possibilities in education. The OU had been using the Internet for a variety of tasks on a number of different courses. Its main use was for computer mediated communication (CMC), which allowed students to communicate with each other, their tutor and staff at the OU. Some courses had begun using the Web in addition to the printed course units, video, multi-media CD ROMs and so forth which go to make up a typical OU course. The Web was a convenient way to offer some material that changed rapidly or would incur cost to distribute, for example student notices and current journal papers.

OU material is produced to a very high standard, and has a deserved reputation for the quality of its print, audio/visual and multi-media material. Such quality comes at a price, however, and within the OU this is reflected in terms of long production cycles, and a large administrative overhead. Typical OU courses take around three years to produce, and usually run for eight years (although they may be updated during this period). This poses something of a problem when working in a rapidly changing field such as computing and IT. The usual response to this is to work at an abstract level: the way computers operate does not change much even if the software we use on them does.

However, we wanted to create a course which had a resonance with the everyday world in which students lived and worked. The course should appeal to a broad range of students and bring them into the culture of computers and the Internet. Such a course needed to be topical, and to feel current to students. A Web based course offered a means of achieving this. An early and fundamental decision was made to make the Web absolutely central to the course. It was not an addition to the usual course components – the Web site effectively *was* the course. This liberated us in a number of ways. First, the OU did not have systems in place to deal with such a course, and so to an extent we could operate outside the normal practice, which removed many of the administrative constraints. Second, through the use of design templates the authors could produce material which was near to the finished article fairly rapidly. This meant we could review and alter it easily. A small, enthusiastic and – importantly – flexible team gathered around the course. There was some scepticism outside of this team regarding the course and whether it would gain any students or tutors willing to work in this manner.

The course was produced in a year along with the requisite tutorial strategy and the technical infrastructure. It was piloted in 1999 with 900 students and 50 tutors; soon students were clamouring to sign on. In 2000 the course was presented twice to meet student demand and there were some 12,000 students registered. This number had to be limited in order to cope with finding the 600 tutors needed to support that number of students. Many of these students and tutors were new to the OU and had signed up specifically because of this course. T171 led to university-wide changes in strategy, student support, organizational structure and course development.

As I have said, I will return to T171 throughout the book, but for now it offers a good demonstration of both the demand for such courses and the impact they can have upon an institution.

Educational technology: promise unfulfilled

I have on my shelf a book whose very title says more about the excessive optimism surrounding new technologies than I can ever express. It is called *CD-ROM – the New Papyrus* (Lambert and Ropiequet, 1986). Such hype is typical for new technologies, and in no area is it seen more keenly than in education. In their proclamations of wonder regarding any new technology, educators often resemble the character Bingo Little in P G Wodehouse. He fell in love, seemingly at random, and each time declared it to be the real thing, and when it was pointed out that this was not the first such occurrence, would deplore the thought that those previous infatuations could be compared to the depth of feeling this time.

There is still no clear evidence that educational technology improves student learning. Tom Russell's (1999) by now famous *The No Significant Difference Phenomenon* compiled all the studies that compared modes of delivery: for example, distance versus classroom, and online versus face to face. The overwhelming conclusion was that the mode of delivery made no difference to student performance, so it is the content and not the medium that seems to be important. However, there are also studies which demonstrate an improved performance using some educational technologies (and indeed the *No Significant Difference* Web site now has a less well populated *Significant Difference* counterpart). As a colleague once commented, this is a case of good news, bad news. The good news is there is no significant difference. The bad news is – there is no significant difference. So if you are a distance educator it undermines any criticism that face to face education is somehow better. However, if you have just invested heavily in new educational technology it might also suggest that there is little gain to be made from this. It should be pointed out that a number of people (eg Phipps and Merisotis, 1999) dispute Russell's findings, arguing that the papers gathered are questionable and thus any conclusions drawn from them are equally inconclusive. Let us, for now, pass over the debate about the impact of technology upon learning achievement. It is the impact upon teaching practice where educational technology seems to have been much less significant than the investment, discussion and optimism surrounding it would warrant. The reasons are varied: for instance, a focus on buying hardware rather than integration, and a lack of training for teachers, undoubtedly contribute to this.

Despite the promise of new technologies, and the excitement that accompanies them, the bulk of educational practice has remained largely unchanged. The face to face lecture is still by far the dominant form of teaching. While computers and various computer based tools may be used to supplement traditional teaching, this can be seen as an extension of the laboratory based classroom. So why, despite a great deal of investment and many innovative, beneficial implementations, is teaching at all levels much the same as it was hundreds of years ago? Is it because the face to face lecture is really the best way of teaching?

Pronouncement of the death of the traditional lecture always seems to be a consequence of a new technology, and yet it persists stubbornly. Personally, I have a lot of time for the lecture. When done well it really is an engaging and inspiring experience. So why are so many people seemingly anxious for its demise? The truth is that it is all too often far from an engaging or inspiring experience. We have all sat through lectures that seemed to have no direction, and resembled an unconnected series of words from which you could fathom no meaning. The repeatability and quality assurance of a lecture is difficult to ensure. Technology is seen as a means of improving productivity, efficiency and reliability. There are also other factors that often combine, making the need for investment in educational technology seem unavoidable. I shall look at these in more detail later, where the motivations for adopting an online approach are examined.

In this chapter I want to look at some previous educational technologies, and analyse why these failed to have the impact on education once predicted, and why the Net will have a more significant impact. The two previous technologies I will use by way of example are broadcast media and multi-media CD ROM.

Broadcast media and CD ROM

The advent of radio, and later television, saw much interest in their use as educational technologies. The term 'University of the Airwaves' began to be used in the 1920s, and in 1951 the Pennsylvania 'University of the Air' began broadcasting lectures. When the OU was first conceived in the 1960s, it was described in similar terms. However, very early on, the OU realized that simply broadcasting lectures did not make for an effective educational experience. Instead it developed an approach to distance learning based primarily around specifically written printed materials, supported by face to face tutorials, summer schools and home experiment kits. The television and radio components formed one element of this overall package, but far from its most significant one. Most audio/visual material tends to act as a supplement to traditional print materials, which are carefully constructed to be unambiguous, complete and understandable (attributes which cannot always be ascribed to a lecture).

While it is true that audio/visual material can greatly enhance the learning experience, it has failed to become the primary delivery method for distance education material. Merely watching or listening to the lecture at a distance does not make for a rewarding educational experience, for a number of reasons relating to the nature of the face to face lecture. First, watching a broadcast or a video of a lecture is a very passive activity. When attending a lecture one is participating in an experience, often in a subtle manner, since it is not the explicit interaction that may be found in a smaller tutorial session. The lecturer may react to the audience, changing what he or she intended to say, relaxing after a joke gets a good response, or going over an explanation again when encountering a sea of blank faces. The members of the audience also have a connection with each other, and will see how others are reacting to the lecture. None of these subtle interactions occur with the broadcast lecture.

Second, the lecture does not occur in isolation. There is often informal discussion afterwards in coffee bars and corridors. Lastly, the lecture is a one to many relationship, whereas watching a lecture at a distance is a one to one connection. The manner of speaking is thus inappropriate: after all, one would not speak to a single student in a tutorial in the same style as giving a lecture. The overall result of this is that the student whose education is merely watching lectures at a distance is not, and does not feel, a participant in the educational experience. In their book *Situated Learning* (1991) Lave and Wenger propose the notion of legitimate peripheral participation as a means of learning. The idea here is that people learn in a social context by partaking in activities which are legitimate: that is, meaningful to the community, although not central. I would suggest that merely watching broadcast lectures is not a legitimate activity in the context of the learning experience. The student does not engage with the material or with the learning community.

In the late 1980s the rise of the personal computer and CD ROMs saw a growth in the use of multi-media computer based training (CBT) or computer assisted learning (CAL) packages, which seemed to offer a solution to some of the problems educators faced both at a distance and on campus. These problems included student motivation, supply and use of laboratory equipment, the explanation of complex processes and coping with the rise in student numbers. Multimedia CD ROMs allowed manufacturers to provide engaging, attractive software, which could incorporate simulations, audio, video (to a limited extent) and animations, as well as straightforward text and images. Through the use of interactive simulations, students could see the effects of different parameters on complex processes, which could make the implications of dry mathematical equations come alive for engineers, say. Or the complexities of Joyce's *Ulysses* could be brought to life and explained with sub-explanations of the numerous references, video clips of Dublin, audio of Joyce speaking, and so on. And it was all in one neat package: there was no need to stop reading the printed unit, dig out the tape recorder for the audiocassette, or watch the video. In addition, the CD could be made available to all students, so some of the tutorial time could be replaced by CD use.

It still sounds ideal, and there are many good educational CDs in circulation, but it is true to say that their use has not quite had the impact upon education across all sectors that was originally envisaged. Most schools will have a collection of CDs, but often they remain unused or only partially incorporated into lessons. In higher education they have been used successfully in a number of distance education courses, but again their role has largely been that of supplement to the core material. They have rarely become the course itself. On campus their role is largely one of reference material, housed in the library. Again it is rare for their content to be integrated deeply into a series of lectures. In the next section some of the reasons behind this lack of uptake will be examined by way of comparison with the Net.

Why the Net is different

Since I have painted a gloomy picture regarding the impact of educational technology up to this point, why should you assume the use of the Net will be any different? The simple answer is that you should not. It could be, but equally if it is not implemented carefully it will struggle to reach its potential. There are a number of mitigating factors in favour of the Net in education, however, which indicate that its place as an educational technology may be more significant than those mentioned above. I will examine these five factors now.

1   Social acceptance

The first factor in the Net's favour is that, in terms of everyday usage, it has already reached a greater penetration in society than most other educational technologies (with the exception of broadcast technologies). Its profile is high and it is the subject of huge financial investment from major corporations who are keen to make the Net central to their strategy. So it is not going to go away, and increasingly it is a medium through which many people perform everyday functions, such as booking their holidays, buying their groceries, contacting their children at college and diagnosing medical ailments. It does not need to be the case that everyone does everything through the Net, but as De Kare-Silver (1998) points out, a small shift, say of 15 per cent, of customers is enough to have a major impact on many businesses. So, as with undecided voters in marginal electoral seats, their influence can go far beyond their actual numbers.

De Kare-Silver calculates that by averaging all the predictions of when the Internet will be an accepted mainstream technology for Western society as a whole, one should estimate that 2005 will be the point of major acceptance. This means that by this time a large percentage of the population will be performing a significant proportion of their daily activities (shopping, communicating, leisure activities, etc) via the Internet. It would perhaps be foolish to assume that in such a climate people will not expect to have their education via the same means.

So whereas CD ROMs offered a convenient and often attractive means of providing educational software, they were doing so largely in the context of a society with ambivalence towards the technology. Apart from games and occasionally consulting a CD encyclopaedia, the CD ROM did not have a large impact upon the daily lives of many people. This is not true of the Net, which is transforming almost every aspect of commerce and services. One is not struggling to convince an audience of the potential of the technology, but operating in an environment that is in a process of rapid take-up. This is a key factor, that much of the drive for use of the Net in education is coming from the 'market'. It is not a technology in which educators alone see the benefit, but rather one where the students themselves have a great deal of experience and enthusiasm for its use. This factor will become increasingly important as the 'Net generation' enters higher education or training.

2 Educator proximity

One might argue that a favourable market might also be said of radio or television, but these have failed to impact upon traditional educational methods. This is true and this brings us to the next key advantage the Net has in being a significant educational technology, that of educator proximity to the finished product. The first aspect of this is one of cost. CDs are expensive to produce, although still achievable, whereas television programmes are beyond the reach of most universities. The production and airtime costs all but rule them out, except where special arrangements exist (such as with the OU and the BBC). Videotape is an affordable option, however, although production quality is limited. I will argue later in this book that producing Web based material is not as cheap as many people would like to believe. However, even with additional input from Web developers and designers, producing a Web based course will probably be cheaper than producing and airing a professional 30-minute television programme or full CD ROM.

There is an issue of scale here also: if the programme, Web based course or CD is to be used by a large number of students, then it justifies a substantial investment. If it is to be used by a relatively small cohort of students, then such investment cannot be justified. Producing a Web site is probably better suited to this small scale delivery. Multi-media CD ROMs are large software undertakings: they require software engineers, graphic designers, project managers, and so forth. For a good insight into the complexities of producing an educational CD, I recommend *I Sing the Body Electronic* by Fred Moody (1996), which gives an account of a year in the life of a CD production team at Microsoft. Because these CDs are such large projects requiring such specialist skills, the educator becomes remote from the process. CDs are produced by companies such as Microsoft or Dorling Kindersley and sold to educators to do with as they will. They are rarely developed by the educators themselves. This means the CD itself may be flawed from an educational design perspective (although many are excellent from this point of view). The teams at Microsoft or wherever will have educational advisers, but they become one element in a team which has many other concerns. Even if the CD is itself well designed from an educational perspective, it is an impersonal product: the educator who has to use it has no personal involvement with it.

Currently educators do not get lost in the mix of media professionals when producing Web material. They still maintain a close proximity to the finished product. This is important for two reasons: the educational input does not get subjugated to the demands of other professionals as easily; and psychologically the educator retains an affinity and a sense of ownership with the material. The finished product is therefore likely to both be better in terms of educational design and have greater backing from the educator involved. The caveat of 'currently' is added here because as Web sites become increasingly complex there is a tendency for them to become more akin to large software or media projects, with the result that increasing levels of intermediary are placed between the educator and the finished product. Maintaining the balance between producing a professional, competent Web site, and retaining the benefits of the medium for the educator is a difficult task. The provision of tools that allow educators to use templates for design and course structure does suggest that much of the emphasis in current Web education environments is on maintaining this educator proximity. Overall then, the Net facilitates a sense of control and therefore ownership for educators far more than previous technologies.

3   Generic interface

This is perhaps an obvious, almost trivial factor, but one that I feel is actually quite significant. One of the problems with CD ROMs is that each one has a different interface, a different structure and navigational method. Each time learners sit down at a new CD they have to learn a new way of interacting. Often this becomes the task in itself. Research has shown that while many teachers are pleased with the content of multi-media CDs, they are frustrated by the navigation and structure (Plowman, 1997). Users often become more focused on finding their way around, and looking for buttons to click, than on the educational material – in short they become focused on surface rather than deep activities. Learning the CD becomes the task in itself.

One advantage of the Web is that the Web browser has become a generic interface. It is true that every Web site has its own navigation structure, but these are wrapped up in the comfortable environment of the Web browser. Whereas a user feels that every CD is a new system to be learnt, they already feel familiar with a Web browser, so do not approach each Web site with the same trepidation. This is related to the first factor, that of social acceptance. Having used the same interface for buying their groceries, doing their banking and sending their e-mails, learners find that using the browser to access educational material removes some of the anxiety about the educational experience itself. The familiar interface acts in some way as a 'comfort blanket', particularly to those who are nervous about study. Similarly, although the Web is a far larger resource than any CD, many users are familiar with finding information in this resource, so the searching, book-marking and navigating processes are all familiar, whereas they are new for each CD.

Another issue for CD usage in education is the vast quantity of information CDs can store. Ironically their great promise is also part of their downfall. They contain a great deal of material, which can often be accessed in a number of ways, and with a variety of paths through this jungle of resource. Pick any educator, from any level, and he or she will tell you that time is one of the biggest constraints. Who has the time to learn the contents of a CD to the extent they would need to in order to really integrate it into lessons? True, in the long term it may actually free up time for them, but the constant pressures on educators mean they rarely have the luxury of being able to consider the long-term benefits. How many schools or universities would buy out an educator's time to allow them to develop a cohesive lesson structure which utilized CDs to their fullest? It is perhaps no surprise that the use of CDs tends to be one of 'Go and see what you can find about the topic', as this does not require the educator to have spent many hours determining the structure and content of the product.

The advent of DVDs means the storage capacity of discs is set to increase dramatically, yet this does not offer a solution for the overworked educator, or indeed the student for whom time will increasingly be the restricting factor in education. In fact, increasing the amount of material by an order of magnitude only means it is more likely to sit neglected in a stock cupboard. In this case more is not necessarily better. There is of course far more information on the Net than can be found on a CD, but equally there are sites that help you through this, from search engines to portals.

4   Interactivity and personalization

The fourth factor that favours the Net as an educational technology is that it is both an interactive and personal medium. Interactivity is one of the key areas where the Net differs from traditional broadcast media. Watching television is essentially a passive, solitary pursuit. Using the Net is an active one, and more significantly it is two-way: the user interacts with other users. In his book Webonomics (1997: 27) Evan Schwartz puts it like this: 'Contrary to what some people believe the Web is not a mass medium. It's a niche medium, a personal medium, and an interactive medium.'

There are certain accepted values which generally go unchallenged as being beneficial in education, including interaction (with each other, the educator, or the learning material), activity (doing something with the information rather than just being a passive recipient) and individualization (all learners are not the same). The Net is well suited to delivering on such matters, whereas television and radio are not. The Net has the potential for enabling communication, whereas many of the previous technologies were primarily concerned with information delivery. The Net can perform this function also, but it is the communication aspect which really sets it apart. Television is about everyone receiving the same information, usually in a passive manner. One does not talk about 'using' television or video, whereas one does talk about using the Net. Television is excellent at some things: for instance, sharing a large sporting event. It is of limited use in education, however. This is an important difference, which many detractors of the Net fail to grasp: the Net is ideally suited to the demands of education, whereas traditional broadcast media are in direct opposition to many of its core values.

5 Sustaining and disruptive technology

This brings me on to the last point as to why the Net is a better contender as an educational technology than many of its predecessors. It is related to the manner in which technology is adopted by organizations, and in turn the impact technology has upon those organizations. I stated earlier that the Net stood a good chance of being a significant technology because implementation of it was occurring in a favourable environment. This is only half the story. The Internet in all its forms is a technology capable of altering organizations. It is not merely that they are keen to adopt it, but also that adoption can completely transform the nature, processes and profile of an organization.

Clayton Christensen (1997) argues that new technologies can broadly be categorized as being one of two types: sustaining or disruptive. His argument goes that the reason many good companies fail is that they spend their time developing, or investing in, sustaining technologies. These are exactly what their existing customers want. The company may be aware of the new disruptive technologies, but the performance of these at the time is often inferior to the existing technology, and crucially their existing customers do not want them. For example, when IBM listened to its mainframe computer customers, their needs were completely different from what the new personal computer could offer. Their customers wanted bigger, better mainframes, not small, flaky PCs which were unsuited to the tasks they performed on a daily basis. The new disruptive technology is thus developed by a new, smaller company (for example Apple), and by the time the larger one realizes the new market and technology are significant it is probably too late. Although IBM created the PC we use today, it did so by setting up an external company, and when it incorporated this back into the parent company it lost the market. It also lost the software market to a then tiny company called Microsoft. Christensen defines the two types of technology thus:

> Most new technologies foster improved product performance. I call these
> sustaining technologies... What all sustaining technologies have in common

is that they improve the performance of established products, along the dimensions of performance that mainstream customers in major markets have historically valued...

Disruptive technologies bring to a market a very different value proposition than had been available previously. Generally, disruptive technologies underperform established products in mainstream markets. But they have other features that a few fringe (and generally new) customers value.

(Christensen, 1997: xv)

Multi-media CDs and broadcast technologies could be classified as sustaining technologies in an educational context. They did not severely disrupt the organizations involved, and they did not reach new markets. It is thus unsurprising that their role has remained largely peripheral: that was the role they were born into, in a sense.

The Net is an obvious candidate for a disruptive technology. However, it is not an inherently disruptive technology, but its categorization lies in its use by any organization. A retailer that uses it to supplement its physical shops, for example by home delivery from supermarkets, is using it in a sustaining context. It does not intend Web based shopping to displace its standard retail outlets, but rather it hopes the two will complement each other.

This is the manner in which many in education see the Net at the moment. It can act as a useful sustaining technology in education: for example as an additional resource for students, or as a means of allowing distance students to communicate with each other, or as a way of delivering items which change frequently, such as recommended journal articles, without committing these to print.

It is, however, my contention that such a use of the Net will result in two undesirable outcomes for educational establishments. First, the educators themselves will not come to appreciate its full potential, leaving it to be another almost-ran in the history of educational technology in these institutions. Second, the institutions will lose considerable market to new organizations that offer the types of online courses customers want. These might be private universities, online training companies, corporate universities or individual tutors. Indeed, Christensen lists 'Distance education, typically enabled by the Internet' as a disruptive technology. There is a warning for existing universities and providers of education in Christensen's book, and that is that it is rarely the incumbents who successfully exploit a disruptive technology, but rather new, smaller organizations who are not burdened by much of the baggage inherent in an established method of doing things. We shall look at these trends, opportunities and threats for education in more detail in the next two chapters, but for now it is sufficient to recognize that educational establishments face competition now more than they have ever done.

So my last reason for commending the Net as a survivable educational technology with significant impact is its ability to function as a disruptive technology, which both alters the organization in which it is implemented, and reaches a very different audience.

Lessons for implementation

Having stated some reasons for having some faith in the Net to deliver as an educational tool, I should now add a caveat, which is somewhat circular: the Net can be an effective educational technology only when it is employed properly.

What do I mean by 'properly'? In my opinion there are some key factors that determine how successfully an educator or university adopts it. These issues will be returned to and expanded upon in the remainder of this book.

1   Do not implement it as a mass medium

This may upset some managers who see the Net as a cheap method of increasing their educator-to-student ratio, but merely using the Net as a distribution mechanism misses one of its key points. Since we have learnt that merely broadcasting lectures over the airwaves is not a meaningful educational experience, it is somewhat surprising to see many people making the same mistake with the Web. Just as television programme makers soon discovered that good television drama was not achieved by pointing a camera at a stage play, so online educators need to find ways of using the new medium effectively. It is a two-way medium and this is what makes it ideal for use as an educational technology. This also means you cannot just put up course notes and disappear for a semester.

2   Do not adopt it in isolation

As we saw with multi-media CDs, merely delivering the technology to educators and sitting back waiting for magic does not produce results. If an organization intends to adopt an Internet based approach then it needs to do so across all its processes. The Net will remain a peripheral technology if a student can take a Web based course but has to telephone the administration and request a form to reserve a place on a course. At the institutional level the Net needs to be implemented across all its units. As an educator you may not have the time or influence to effect such change, but that should not deter you from implementing an online course. You should adopt the same principle, and that is to integrate the Net into the philosophy of the course. This means rethinking every aspect of the course, including delivery of materials, the content students have access to, the pedagogy underlying the course, its assessment and the social significance for students. This is in essence what this book hopes to address: the complete range of considerations that the Net brings to education.

3 Be prepared to experiment and change

Be prepared to try different learning approaches, and then modify them next year. The Net is a very new and fluid medium, so you should never expect to have a course set in stone. It will always be changing and adapting. This is both exciting and terrifying. As an educator it is important not to be shackled by what one might term 'the tyranny of training'. This is seen particularly with relevance to IT training. Many people feel they cannot do something or use a package until they have had the appropriate training. Nothing makes you learn a new technology as fast as having to use it. So develop a prototype, pick up your skills as you go along.

If the Net does nothing more, it will have been a valuable tool if it promotes a culture of self-reflection in educators and restores a sense of fun to education. It is often difficult to experiment in an educational context, because we are dealing with the education of real people. I am not arguing that you should not think carefully about the course and the student experience, but you should not become paralysed because of a desire to create the perfect learning experience the first time around. Most of us can remember the painful experience of giving our first lectures. We improve in that arena, so if we are prepared to accept improvement in performance in the face to face environment, then why not in the virtual one? The enthusiasm and input which educators give to their first steps into online learning can more than compensate for any initial hiccups.

4 Make the Net central to the course

The reasons for doing this are twofold. First, do so for the good of the course itself. It is only by placing the Net at the centre of the course that you will fully utilize all that it offers. If you make it an additional component among many others, then students will treat it as you have done: as a peripheral element. Unsurprisingly, in such an implementation you will find it used relatively little. If the educator is to gain from using the Net, then it must be at the expense of other components, otherwise it becomes yet another time-consuming task. If students are to gain from what the Net offers, then it should be as a single environment where they can find the information they need and through which they can interact and engage with the material and other students. This will not happen if it stays on the periphery of the course and both parties have a component that takes up time and energy for little reward. Second, it is only by making the Net central to what they do that educators will come to terms with it and be able to compete against new organizations that are keen to embrace the Net as a disruptive technology.

Conclusion

The promise of educational technology has often gone unfulfilled. The Net offers a number of possible advantages over some of the technologies that have gone before. These are partly a result of its ease of use, its penetration in society, but mainly because it is essentially a communication medium. It has the potential to alter the way in which organizations operate and perform many of their tasks, but this brings its own set of problems and challenges.

In the next chapter I will take a broad view of the impact the Internet is having on education, and the possibilities, threats and issues this means universities, colleges and schools are having to face today.

Summary

In this chapter I have looked at the promise of previous educational technology, particularly broadcast media and multi-media CDs. These have not transformed teaching practice in the way they initially promised. I have suggested five reasons why the Net may have a more significant impact:

- social acceptance;
- educator proximity;
- generic interface;
- interactivity and personalization;
- potential as a disruptive technology.

Lastly, I outlined four lessons that I believe both institutions and individual educators should bear in mind when implementing online learning:

- Do not implement it as a mass medium.
- Do not adopt it in isolation.
- Be prepared to experiment and change.
- Make the Net central to the course.

Chapter 2

Exploring some of the e-learning myths

Introduction

When one talks about the Net and education there are a number of other issues, which seem to be related, if not intertwined. These include the globalization and commercialization of education, the quality of education, the merits of distance versus campus based learning, and the very nature of learning institutions themselves. The suggestion often seems to be that these are forces that are inevitable once the technology is used in any form. There are often emotive arguments on both sides, for like all significant technologies the Internet seems to be the battle-field on which a number of other campaigns are going to be waged. There is nothing particularly new in much of this. It is now something of a cliché, but much the same was said of the printing press as is said of the Internet. Dale Spender (1998) sums it up like this:

> Once the printers of the 15th and 16th centuries started to produce books that would sell... the establishment of the day was outraged by this form of catering to the masses. This lowering of standards.
>
> Today we might call the works that were then being printed the 'classics', but when the early printers produced their translations of the ancient Greek and Latin tales, the church called them the corrupting pagan texts which would lead astray the entire population. If books were to get into the hands of the masses, they argued, dangerous ideas would spread, the work of the devil would have free reign – it would be the end of control and the triumph of anarchy.
>
> And there is nothing derogatory that has been said about television today

– or about the dangers of the computer society – that was not said then about the book, and the humanities and classics, when they first made their appearance.

In this chapter I examine some of the commonly expressed beliefs about what the Internet may mean for education, and the reasoning behind these beliefs. First, a word on terminology. The term 'university' is used in this section, since many of the articles that have made claims about the impact of the Net on education have addressed the issue at the level of the university. However, the same issues apply to all forms of higher educational establishment, including further education and community colleges. Primary and secondary education are somewhat removed from the competitive environment, although there is some relevancy here too.

The Internet will mean the commercialization of education

December 2000: an agreement between India and China is announced to oppose the commercialization of education at all fora, stating that education should not be controlled by market forces and that the goal of education should be to create a non-violent and non-exploitative knowledge society. What this news indicated was that the commercialization of education is now a serious, global concern and that it calls into question the very purpose of education in society. So is the commercialization of education inevitable? Is it necessarily a detrimental force? And, what has the Internet to do with it?

The commercialization of education seems to be an attack on the last bastion of the public sector. For many, the role of private companies in health care was, and still is, unacceptable. Yet there is no doubt it has happened, to a greater or lesser extent, depending on where you live. So, it would be naïve perhaps to think that education is in a more privileged position and the same could not happen in that domain. Indeed, venture capitalists now eye the education sector covetously and see it as the next big target. In the year 2000 some $2.9 billion of venture capital was invested in education and training start-up companies (Eduventures.com, 2001). True, the e-commerce bust has seen this investment slow somewhat and some of the shine has come off the optimism, but the sector is still attracting a good deal of finance and attention. There is certainly more drive and, significantly, more money behind the move to involve commercial organizations in education than there ever has been before. And large sums of money tend to have a way of fashioning the output those behind the money desire.

There are a number of reasons that education and commercialization make for an uneasy marriage. Many of the models and practices applicable in business do not transfer easily to education. For instance, the notion of students as customers is fraught with uneasy implications in education. In a commercial relationship customers are not assessed as they are in education, they cannot fail as they do in education. The idea that 'the customer is always right' would make marking any form of assessment very difficult. The notion of academic freedom is similarly difficult to marry with a commercial approach. Commercial pressures and constraints could seriously threaten this liberty. These are wider issues, however, and beyond the scope of this book. I want to focus here on the role the Internet plays in this debate.

Let us be clear before we apportion blame to the Net: it did not start this process. Global cultural changes have meant educational establishments have generally become more accountable and more businesslike in the way they operate. Despite the reservations mentioned above, the 'customer centred' approach has been adopted by many universities in response to a broader customer culture. Many vice-chancellors would argue that they have to operate as a business now, but do so in an unusual market which is much at the whim of governments and politicians. One could view many of the established educational practices as evolving not from pedagogical or student support considerations, but rather as sound economical models. Ellington, Percival and Race (1993: 64) for example say of the traditional lecture, 'one of the reasons why the lecture has retained its dominant place in the educational and training scene is that the method appears to be highly cost-effective, since it enables high student/staff ratios to be achieved'. Online education, because it requires changes to established models of teaching, support, assessment and use of technology, naturally forces universities to examine the financial viability of such a model. This does not mean that it is any more (or less) concerned with profit than traditional forms of education, but rather that we have become so accustomed to these assumptions in the established processes that often we do not notice them.

Gaining access to the education market was always difficult for commercial organizations. The process of becoming an accredited university that can award degrees varies between countries, but is nearly always difficult and protracted. This gives private universities a problem: they need a successfully working educational establishment in order to gain accreditation powers, and yet few students will want to study at a place that is not accredited. The private university needs to employ academic staff and have a campus in operation all the time that it is going through this process. Unlike for other businesses there seems to be little chance of starting small and building up gradually, using the previous year's profits to sustain growth. With a private university the organization has to go directly to the fully established model. This requires some brave and considerable financial backing. Hence the number of private universities has remained relatively small.

The Net changes some of these dynamics. First, because the students and the academics are not located physically on campus, an online university does not need to invest vast sums of money in building a campus with specialized rooms for lecturing, laboratory space, social areas, and so on. It will need a headquarters, but any standard office space will suffice for this. Second, again as a corollary of the academics being located anywhere, there is no need to employ them full-time. A wide range of courses can be offered by employing academics on a part-time basis to deliver the courses online. This is precisely what the University of Phoenix has done in the United States (with greater or lesser success, depending on your point of view). Last, because the costs are lowered by these factors, the online university can appeal to students as an economical means of study, particularly if they wish to study part-time while working and cannot attend a campus based university. So the online university can appeal to a different group of students on different grounds, whereas the private campus-based university was competing directly with the traditional universities. The online university still has to negotiate successfully the rigorous accreditation process, and it will have to invest a lot of money in its technical infrastructure and in marketing, but it begins to appear as a more attractive and viable business model for investors. The Net therefore can lower the cost of entry to the market, although in the next chapter we will see that this is not always borne out – but for now let us assume it does.

However, it may not be the private, online universities that offer the biggest threat to traditional ones. It may be the provision of courses offered by companies that do not claim to be universities, but instead offer courses they feel are of interest. Publishers are a good example of an industry that has previously been complementary to the education sector, which now might become a competitor. They have large quantities of educational content, substantial financial backing and an appreciation of the market. The Net blurs the boundaries between industries, which previously had clearly defined roles, hence the mergers or collaborations between companies in different sectors such as entertainment, publishing, software and finance in Web based ventures. A book used to stand alone, and although autodidacts could educate themselves from these resources alone, most people required some help in understanding the issues and guidance in selecting the relevant texts. What education provides is a cognitive framework within which academic content makes sense. However, if publishers start placing the contents of numerous books online they may decide they need to add value over the printed text. They might also add some multi-media, and crucially, some form of support which weaves together two or more books into a coherent framework. So when does this become a course?

The sorts of courses such companies might offer could be standard training ones (eg 'Basic Web page design') or staff development courses (eg 'French for business'), but they might also be more general interest courses (eg 'Understanding *Hamlet*'). While these might not compete directly for students wanting to gain a first degree, they will compete for those wanting to study for career development or for self-improvement. This is the 'lifelong learning' market that has been much talked about. People who want to study for such reasons may well not want to attend a campus, and may not be interested in gaining an academic qualification (they may well have one of these already). They will choose their course based on the appeal of its content. And if they can choose from a hundred different courses offered worldwide which meet their needs, then the kudos attached to a university offering may not be a sufficient draw.

Naturally, many academics will argue that universities should not be entering the training market, and there is some truth in this. There is usually a mismatch in expectations on both sides when universities offer students training courses. However, the distinction between training and academic-level courses becomes less clear-cut with some areas. In addition, it is surrendering a large part of the function of universities to admit there is an educational need for adults in society, but it is not their remit to meet it. There are many universities and colleges that would see this as part of their role.

Online providers of such courses thus represent a real threat, not only in terms of taking away some of the 'market' from universities and colleges, but also to the perception that the traditional universities and colleges are the sole providers of higher education. If students take courses from private online organizations and find they meet their needs, then it begins to threaten the monopoly of higher education which state universities have enjoyed. This might be what is behind much of the angst directed at the Net from some educators. But is it necessarily a detrimental development? With their experience and expertise, universities should be able to offer an educational experience which will rival anything the private organizations can provide. If state universities find they are losing students to the offerings of commercial organizations, then that surely should indicate that they need to change their own offerings.

This is why the Net is a significant issue in the argument about the commercialization of education. It facilitates the arrival of new providers and allows all educators potentially to reach new audiences. It is in an attempt to meet both of these challenges that the management at many universities are considering alliances with commercial organizations.

The Internet will mean the globalization of education

The Net can be a place of paradox. Within it, seemingly contrary trends can be realized simultaneously, and it can be viewed as the means of achieving diametrically opposing views. This seems particularly pertinent with the arguments about the globalization of education. At one conference I attended, a speaker warned of the threat of a global super-university, while at another conference in South America, someone spoke passionately about the possibility of the Net as a means of educating the populace, so that they might compete with 'the colossus of the north'. So for some, the global aspect of the Net will mean that there will be a few dominant organizations that deliver online education, while for others, the Net is a means to offer good-quality education to a large populace, and begin to compete more effectively in the global economy. There is an element of truth in both of these views.

One of the problems people have on the Net is with finding a reliable provider of any commodity they are seeking. They are either overwhelmed by irrelevant search results, or they find providers they have never heard of and are unsure they can trust. In such an environment a familiar brand name becomes invaluable. On the Net, the brand becomes as important as the location for traditional businesses.

This could have implications for education. If someone is searching for a course, say an online MBA, then rather than filter through lots of results and try to assess the quality of the offerings, there is a temptation to go straight to a known and trusted provider, let us say Harvard. Not only can you guess the appropriate URL (www.harvard.edu), but also you can be assured that the MBA will meet certain standards. In such a scenario the big-name educational establishments (Oxford, Cambridge, Stanford, MIT, etc) become online brand names, to the detriment of many smaller, more local providers. This is the anti-competition scenario where there are ultimately a few, or even only one, online providers, a sort of Microsoft of education.

The alternative view is that in fact students want a course or qualification that is accredited, and thus recognized, in their own country. There are also strong cultural differences between nations that make few subjects generalizable to the extent that they could be studied in any country equally effectively. By utilizing their familiarity with the local culture, the needs, interests and concerns of the environment in which they operate, local universities and colleges can provide a much better online course than a global provider. They might also take advantage of their geographical location, for instance by supporting online courses with face to face activities such as residential schools or day sessions. By operating this way, the local universities can increase the proportion of the population they can educate effectively.

It is likely that neither extreme view will materialize: this is usually the way with new technologies. They encourage visions of technological utopia or dystopia, which often seem to have a determinist underpinning: that is, the technology will force the change, for better or worse, regardless of people. It is the opposite effect – the manner in which technology itself is adapted through use by people – that results in these predictions largely being unfulfilled. When the personal computer first began to achieve a mass audience, the utopians similarly predicted that it would be a democratizing force, which would free the artistic creativity of individuals and give them powerful information tools. The dystopians predicted that it would increase the power of governments and corporations and that people would stop communicating and become slaves to their computers. Of course, neither vision quite came true, and although huge changes occurred in work practices, education and society, it is also true that a great deal stayed the same; we merely found different ways of doing it. From the explosion in computer gaming to the people who transformed their Apple Macintoshes into fish tanks, the technology was used in unexpected and unpredictable ways.

Courses being offered to a global audience raise several issues. The first, and most obvious, is applicability of content. However sensitive to different cultures we might be, we are all influenced by our own environment. It is often difficult to appreciate how relevant the examples you have selected might be in another culture, or whether your use of language contains subtle cultural references that might have different meanings elsewhere. To make the course feel relevant to students you might need to provide local examples or case studies. However, such issues can be addressed, for example by collaboration with a local education establishment, or by careful use of language and a resource bank of different examples.

A more difficult problem to overcome for global courses is the difference in cultural values embodied in the pedagogy. These often go deep to the heart of the social values of a particular culture. For instance, intensive online collaboration is more difficult in a society which tends to promote politeness and reservation. Similarly, strongly familial societies often place a great emphasis on respect, which is also exhibited to teachers. A course pedagogy that expects critical questioning and dialogue with the educator might thus not translate well into such an environment, where such behaviour is usually frowned upon. These factors, combined with language, local recognition and subsidies, suggest that the globalization of education is an issue that will occur only in specific sectors, and usually through collaboration between international partners.

The Internet will mean the death of the campus university

In his thoughtful article 'Electronics and the dim future of university' (1995), Eli Noam argued that:

> While new communications technologies are likely to strengthen research, they will also weaken the traditional major institutions of learning, the universities. Instead of prospering with the new tools, many of the traditional functions of universities will be superseded, their financial base eroded, their technology replaced and their role in intellectual inquiry reduced.
>
> *(Noam, 1995: 247)*

He outlines three main functions of universities: the creation of knowledge (research); the storage of knowledge (libraries); and the transmission of knowledge (teaching). He argues that the new communication technologies alter the economics of each of these functions, thereby undermining the role of the university. For instance, teaching will be undermined because, for the reasons mentioned above, online providers can offer cheaper alternatives. Noam claims that:

> It is hard to imagine that the present low-tech lecture system will survive...
> If alternative instructional technologies and credentialing systems can be devised, there will be a migration away from classic campus based higher education. The tools for alternatives could be video servers with stored

lectures by outstanding scholars, electronic access to interactive reading materials and study exercises, electronic interactivity with faculty and teaching assistants, hypertext books and new forms of experiencing knowledge, video- and computer-conferencing, and language translation programs. While it is true that the advantages of electronic forms of instruction have sometimes been absurdly exaggerated, the point is not that they are superior to face-to-face teaching (though the latter is often romanticized), but that they can be provided at dramatically lower cost.

(Noam, 1995: 248)

This does suggest an underlying model of education merely as information transfer, so again the idea that video lectures will make the face to face version redundant is proposed. However, Noam is arguing that it is not whether we think that this is a good form of education or not that is significant, but rather that it can be a much cheaper form which might be the deciding factor. There might be some truth in this, but students of such courses might soon find them unfulfilling. The notion that the Net represents an infinite lecture hall, with no additional costs for additional students, is a mistaken one. I will discuss issues of scale in a later chapter, but in order to provide a meaningful educational experience, and one that is liable to be repeated by students, the provider needs to give guidance and support. So Noam argues that 'a curriculum, once created, could be offered electronically not just to hundreds of students nearby but to tens of thousands around the world' (Noam, 1995: 248). While it is possible to offer such a course, if it is to be a meaningful education experience it will require a great deal of academic support, which many of the cheaper alternatives would not be able to supply.

What underlies much of Noam's analysis is the physical aspect of universities. Much of their functionality is bundled with this physical realization. So universities were renowned for having a good library, or excellent laboratory facilities, or a pleasant campus – all physical attributes. As Noam points out, the very reason universities came into existence was because of this bundling of knowledge and its physical embodiment. When the early libraries stored knowledge in the form of books, the cost of reproducing books was high, so it made financial sense for those people with an interest in a topic to congregate around these libraries. From this gathering of knowledgeable people universities grew, as others came to be taught by them.

Evans and Wurster (2000) argue that physical objects and information have different sets of economics. They have been forced to follow the same economic model, however, because they have been bound together physically. For example, in a supermarket the information about a product is in the product itself. If I want to look through the range of cereals offered I physically walk the aisle looking at the products themselves. The Internet allows these two aspects to become unbundled. I can browse through a vast collection of books at Amazon, while the actual books can be stored in an out-of-town warehouse.

In educational terms this can be seen as the campus versus distance education debate. Distance education has been implemented successfully before the advent of the Net, but it is with the Net that many universities and colleges have entered the distance education market. There has been a dramatic rise in the number of distance education courses and students over the past few years: for example from 1995 to 1998 there was an estimated 72 per cent increase in distance education programs in the US (Phipps and Merisotis, 2000). As with establishing private universities, the Net lowers the cost of entrance to this market. Delivering distance education used to require specially printed teaching materials, audio/visual components and a face to face network for support. These are costly to develop unless an institution is making a large-scale venture into distance education. The Net allows distance courses to be developed quickly and often on a small scale.

This ultimately leads to the question, 'If all of the functionality of a university can be delivered at a distance, then is there the need for the expensive campus?' In Evans and Wurster's terms, if the separate information and physical economics are uncoupled, then they are free to follow their own paths. The 'university' no longer needs to have a large campus in the middle of a city. Instead it can have an administrative centre in a less expensive area without the need for halls of residence, lecture halls, libraries and so on.

Will all campus universities disappear, then? This depends on a wider social movement. In an interview published in *Forbes*, 27 February 1995, George Gilder predicted that information technologies would lead to the 'death of cities'. His reasoning is much the same as I have outlined above – cities developed out of economic necessity. Industry needed to be near a resource, such as a port, and then the people who worked in or offered services related to that industry needed to be in its close proximity. Now much of the work that people need to do in a knowledge economy can be done at a distance using the Net. There is less and less reason to be located physically near your employer (or even to have one single employer at all). Thus people will be free to live where they choose.

The reason I think this does not necessarily lead to the death of cities is that many people choose to live in them. Their nature might change, but cities have a social inertia, which is its own justification. The same can be said of the campus university. There is, after all, more to a university education than just the degree. A university education is a social experience, often a pivotal one for students. As the former Open University Vice-Chancellor, Sir John Daniel (2000), commented, 'I often argue that university campuses will always be in demand because they create a protected environment where young people can come to terms with life, love, liquor and learning – while sparing the rest of the community the sight of these often unsightly processes'. There is a lot of truth in this: most students will name the social aspect of university life as one of the most significant elements of their overall experience. However, if this is the only advantage large campus universities offer, then it might not be sufficient for the additional costs they entail. There are other ways of having a good time, after all: for instance, a year travelling the world might fulfil a similar function.

An additional advantage of campus based study is the inherent discipline and structure it provides for students. Studying at a distance requires a good deal of self-discipline and organization, in order to manage the time for study against competing demands. Much of this organizational function is provided for students on campus, for instance with timetabled lectures, tutorials and so on, and the culture of academic discipline within which students are situated. Universities should not take the benefits of a campus experience for granted, but equally it is liable to remain a desirable option for a proportion of students.

In offering distance education it could be argued that universities are contributing to their own demise by providing a good educational experience without the need to attend the campus. An alternative view is that in so doing they strengthen their position. Places that offer a mixed or hybrid means of study might well meet the flexible demands of education in the modern world. Students can study part-time for some of their degree, but also attend campus for a period to gain the benefits of a face to face environment. Such study programmes might decrease some of the cost of education and also open it out to members of society who cannot afford three to four years' full-time study. Using the Net in this way increases the reach of the campus university while simultaneously taking advantage of its benefits as a physical institution.

Noam ends his essay by suggesting that universities need to change the roles they perform and make a virtue of their social function. I would concur with this. Universities may have to adapt the services they offer. For instance, students may well adopt a more modular approach to studying, selecting different courses from different providers. Someone studying English literature might take an online course in Shakespeare's tragedies from Oxford, a course in 17th-century literature and culture from Warwick, another on narrative forms from Harvard, and so on (this is hypothetical, by the way: none of these universities offers these courses online for single study yet). Yet another university might provide the overall accreditation of these courses into a named degree, in conjunction with a final-year project. These courses might be chosen from a central Web site which acts as the intermediary between the student and the vast number of courses on offer. This service might be provided by another university, a private company or a government initiative. It is the Net that makes this competition possible. By adapting their procedure to allow courses to be taken in isolation, the universities can make a virtue of specialization, since it can be accommodated in an enormously wide range of offerings from other providers.

It is not the case that all functions of universities will be superseded by other organizations, but these functions do now face competition in a way they never have before. In short, the monopoly is over, and universities will have to adapt to these changes if they are to survive. This might not necessarily be to the detriment of society as many educators portray it. Such changes in education might open it up to many more participants who are currently disadvantaged by the

universi   nt also force educators to critically address the quality
of the'   that has not always been necessary.

7   .l mean declining standards in education

              id 2001 historian David Noble published a series of articles
            ctive heading of *Digital Diploma Mills*. The thrust of the articles
          internet was leading to the commercialization of education and a
         .andards. It was to be resisted at all costs. The articles provoked much
         .it they are deeply flawed in a number of respects. The main arguments
         .n addressing here since they represent many of the objections to online
       .ion, particularly with regard to the quality of education.

 Noble's first claim is that administrators and managers are forcing online
distance education on academics and students. He asks, 'What is driving this
headlong rush to implement new technology with so little regard for deliberation
of the pedagogical and economic costs and at the risk of student and faculty
alienation and opposition?' On the contrary, my experience is that anyone who
has developed an online course has spent far longer thinking about pedagogy and
reflecting on the success of that course than many face to face lecturers. I would
also argue that it is naïve to think that this is being forced upon students against
their will. As T171 attests, many students are keen to study this way and are
comfortable with the technology. Although there is resistance from many academics to engaging with the Net, there is also a great deal of enthusiasm and
excitement about the possibilities it creates. Many universities are attempting to
create a pedagogical and technical framework to meet these demands from
educators and students.

Noble's next main claim is that the Net will lead to the commoditization of
education. He claims, 'Once faculty put their course material online, moreover,
the knowledge and course design skill embodied in that material is taken out of
their possession, transferred to the machinery and placed in the hands of the
administration.' This seems to assume a very simplistic pedagogic model, which
again views education as merely information transfer. This would be the case if
the video lecture were an effective distance learning model, but as I have argued
elsewhere, it is not. We will explore online pedagogies in more detail later, but
good online courses all have an element of communication, interaction and
support. This is what the academic brings to the educational experience. If, as
Noble is suggesting, it were just a matter of content, then the book would have
replaced lecturers long ago.

The last of his claims that I will address here is that the Net will increase
distance education, which inevitably means a lowering of education standards.
This is little more than snobbery about the value of face to face education. He
states that distance educators 'have been compelled to reduce their instructional
costs to a minimum, thereby undermining their pedagogical promise. The

invariable result has been not only a degraded labor force but a degraded product as well. The history of correspondence education provides a cautionary tale in this regard, a lesson of a debacle hardly heeded by those today so frantically engaged in repeating it.' This is quite an outdated view of distance education as merely 'correspondence tuition'. It is also difficult to square this with the fact that, as we have seen, there is rarely any difference between distance and campus students, and that the quality of distance education offered by many universities is highly rated (for example, the Open University is regularly ranked in the top ten of universities in the UK by the Department of Education).

What was interesting about the articles was the reaction they provoked. A number of academics felt that someone was at last fighting the forces of change, which had been promoted as inevitable. This uncovered some underlying beliefs and anxieties about online education. These anxieties are a serious issue for universities to address. Educators should not feel as though the change is being forced upon them without adequate support and development. We will look at changes within the organization in a later chapter, but staff support was one of the seven key factors identified in a recent report about quality in online education (Phipps and Merisotis, 2000). There is a duty on the part of the institution to support its staff, but equally staff have a duty to engage with new technologies. Many academics who are disparaging about the Net do not engage with it. Academics do not need to become Web developers or experts in using the latest software, but just as they are expected to be able to use a library effectively, they should be able to use the new information tools.

The way to ensure the quality of online education is for educators to become involved with the process, not to refuse to engage with it. There is nothing intrinsic in online education that necessarily leads to a lowering of quality. Indeed, there is probably a great deal more scrutiny of online education than there is of traditional face to face teaching, with the result that there is a greater effort in maintaining its quality. The fear of being replaced by online resources is a misplaced one, I feel. If some video lectures and resources can replace educators, then in all probability the educators deserve to be replaced, since they are not adding much to the educational experience of their students. Most educators do far more than this and can continue to do so online.

The Internet is good for training but not for education

Another view I have heard expressed in various guises is that the Net is a good medium for training, but not for education. For example, Noble says, 'education must be distinguished from training (which is arguably more suitable for distance delivery), because the two are so often conflated'. The notion that the Net is suitable only for training seems to derive from a view of the Net as a delivery mechanism once again, rather than as an interactive medium. The suggestion is that it is good for training because this is about information transfer (although many trainers might disagree with this view also), whereas education is about the creation of knowledge through dialogue and interaction. The rapid growth in the number of commercial organizations offering e-training also seems to support the view that this is the Net's natural level in education. Such courses are often technically accomplished, with well-designed Web sites and professional media, but they can be pedagogically poor, for many of the reasons Noble has cited in *Digital Diploma Mills*. The company needs to maximize profits, and so cannot always offer the intensive support needed. This need not be the same for education, however. The idea that the Net is suitable only for training and not for education only holds true if one thinks of the Net as a one-way mechanism for delivering lectures or other content. As soon as you conceive of the Net as a two-way medium, it becomes ideal for offering supported distance education. Students can interact with the academics and with each other on a flexible basis. In Chapter 10 I will outline a framework for classifying online courses which clarifies the differences between training and higher education courses.

Lessons for implementation

Now we have looked at some of the issues surrounding e-learning, what lessons can be drawn for its implementation? There is no single solution, and much will vary according to the particular characteristics of an institution. But there are some general conclusions we can draw from these broader issues.

1 Be aware of competition

The Net has facilitated the arrival of competition from a variety of sources. It is no longer easy to dismiss these on the basis that they do not provide 'proper' education. With sufficient financial backing and lower overheads, the courses offered by these new providers may well be able to better the current offerings of universities. They may compete on specific characteristics, such as range and attractiveness of courses, or use of technology, or level of support, or simply price. If you are offering an online or campus based course, it is a good idea to see what else is available in that subject area. By familiarizing yourself with what the competition offer you will appreciate where your course stands and how it might differ. From a teaching perspective it is always useful to see how other people are approaching the same subject. There may well be online resources that can be accommodated into your course also. Previously, people might have had some knowledge of courses taught at different universities in the same subject, but there were a number of other factors in determining where students studied, not solely the course. If students can pick and choose different courses from different providers, then the course itself is the granularity at which students will operate, rather than the university or the degree programme. There is therefore a greater requirement to be familiar with other courses.

2 Be adaptable in courses and approach

If the number of courses available to any one student suddenly increases, then the student is liable to make good use of this choice. As the competitive market opens up, courses that are perceived as uninteresting or unlikely to help with employment might no longer find an audience. This is happening already in many areas regardless of online education (for example, engineering subjects are finding it difficult to recruit students in the UK). The move to online provision might well enhance this trend, although conversely, by offering courses to a broader audience a new set of students might be discovered, for example students in a country which still has a strong engineering culture.

If a course is failing to attract students, then it might be time to adapt it (or perhaps just promote it differently). This might be in terms of content, for example making it more current, or it might be in terms of approach, for example altering the pedagogy to make it more interactive.

Institutions as a whole might find that they need to cancel some courses and replace them with courses that are more likely to appeal to the Net audience. I mentioned earlier that the notion of student as customer was an uneasy fit in educational terms, but in the area of customer choice it will probably behave like any other market. If you do not have the 'product' customers want they will go elsewhere.

3 Make a virtue of what you can offer

With many courses available, online students may well look to other factors to influence their choice. Universities offering a mixed approach may appeal to students if the location of the university is attractive, for instance in an interesting city or in a desirable location. There are different interpretations of a mixed approach: for example, it can be a standard undergraduate degree with some courses delivered online; evening tutorials for online courses; residential weeks at the campus; or one or more years spent studying at a distance. In this instance the physical aspect of the university can be an advantage over the online providers. Similarly, the social function of a campus university can be a factor which can be promoted as an additional benefit. In this case the university has to invest a lot in creating the sort of social amenities which can be seen as attractive compared with other offerings. The presence of well-known academics might also be a draw for students. Just as recorded music and live videos have not diminished the attendance at music concerts, so students will still want to attend the live lectures of prominent academics in a subject. This makes a virtue of the face to face lecture as an event in which students participate. It might be that a university deliberately adopts a policy of not providing any online courses. Instead it promotes its face to face lectures and tutorial system as a positive factor. Such a strategy might well find favour with many students, but it would require the university to offer more interaction than is currently available on many campuses. Academics might be encouraged to give engaging lectures, so that the university gains a reputation for the quality of its teaching presentations. Alternatively, the university might promote its online courses through the level of support it offers students, or the currency of its curriculum, or the quality of its teaching materials.

In all of these cases the university is making a decision to promote one or more aspects of what it does as a reason for selecting it over a competitor.

4 Offer flexible programmes

As well as being adaptable at the course level, universities will need to offer more flexible study patterns for students than the standard undergraduate degree programme. As I have already mentioned, this might include offering single courses for study, rather than signing up for a whole degree. It might also be realized through study programmes which allow students to take time out, to study partially at a distance or part-time, to link up with other universities for support and so on. The standard three or four year full-time degree programme will still appeal to many students, but there will be an increasing proportion who want greater flexibility in their study. Most universities have already made steps towards meeting this demand, with deferred or transferred credit for previous study, part-time study programmes, community outreach projects and so forth. The increase in online distance education provision will mean a rise in the demand for such flexibility.

Conclusion

For education, these are the best of times and these are the worst of times. The Internet and associated technologies make this an exciting time to be involved in education. Many of the fundamental assumptions underlying our approach to education have been a product of the physical constraints of colocation. These no longer apply and so many of these assumptions are now being challenged and undermined. This is exciting in that education is liable to see greater change over the next 20 years than has been seen since the foundation of universities removed knowledge from the power of the church. It is also a frightening and worrying prospect because many of the important values embodied in the education system might be weakened by this change. In his insightful book *Code and Other Laws of Cyberspace* (1999), Larry Lessig examines the nature of the Net and possible influences upon its regulation. He repeatedly stresses the importance of both the ability to make choices and the need to make them:

The choices are rich, but they are *choices*.

If we let the invisible hand work unimpeded, these choices will be made according to the set of interests that are expressed by commerce on the Net. In some cases, certainly, those interests will be constrained by government. But now we must think specifically about how we could structure the choices we will confront and how we could resolve the conflicts of values these spaces will present.

Our choices in each case are two. We can try to make cyberspace the same as real space, investing it with the same values, or we can give cyberspace values and properties that are fundamentally different.

(Lessig, 1999: 83)

Educators are in much the same position with regards to the Net. Lessig was talking about rights, the constitution of the Net, but all of the above could equally apply to education. This is a time of change, and by engaging in that change educators can fashion the choices that are made. If they do not engage with it, then these choices will still be made, but by people other than educators.

As anyone who has watched children use the Net will know, this technology is going to have a significant impact upon society. Children demonstrate little fear of using the technology, use it for all manner of research and communication, and have been responsible for the rise in popularity of many applications, for example instant messaging. The Net changes the way people communicate and who they communicate with, it alters the type of information available and who publishes it, and it removes barriers of distance. I would argue that educators have a duty to engage with such a social change, particularly one that has such a potential in education and to meet the needs of their students. To merely resist the change on the basis of fear or prejudice is to fail in the role of universities within society. I started the chapter with a quote from Dale Spender, so let me end with one from her too. In talking about the impact of the Net on education she suggested that:

The end of the 19th century witnessed the democratization of reading. It was a time when schools taught literacy, when libraries were established, where people were so encouraged to take up reading that it led to the growth of the mass audience – and the belief in books as a good thing. But at the end of the 20th century, we are witnessing the democratization of authorship. Where it is open to everyone with an internet account to become an author, to make their own meanings, from email to web sites.

(Spender, 1998)

Personally, I think it would be a shame if the educators of today excluded themselves from this process.

I have attempted to dispel some of the accusations regarding the dangers that e-learning poses for education as a whole. This is not to say that it will not have a profound effect, though. The Net will lead to increased competition, and it will mean that many universities and educators have to change the way they have operated for many years. This is the same sort of change that will be occurring in many parts of society, particularly business. The change in these sectors is probably in advance of that in education. For this reason I will look at what lessons can be drawn from e-business in the next chapter.

Summary

In this chapter the following issues surrounding the Internet and education have been examined:

- the commercialization of education;
- the globalization of education;
- the potential demise of the campus university;
- the role the Net plays in a perception of declining standards in education;
- the suggestion that online delivery is suitable for training purposes and not education.

From this, four lessons were drawn for implementation:

- Be aware of competition.
- Be adaptable in courses and approach.
- Make a virtue of what you can offer.
- Offer flexible programmes.

Chapter 3

Lessons from e-commerce

Introduction

In the last chapter we looked at some of the issues surrounding the Net and education. One significant factor was the arrival of new competitors in education. A consequence of this is that education becomes referred to in increasingly commercial terms. It begins to be viewed as a product, the students as a market, and educational institutions as organizations with the same pressures as commercial ones. Depending on your point of view this may just be a practical and realistic view, or it may be the start of an insidious process. The Net seems to facilitate this process, and many institutions are wondering how to adapt to this changing environment. The commercial sector has been forced to engage with the Net through the arrival of new e-commerce operations and the need to maintain a competitive advantage. This has entailed the development of new working practices, organizational change and new commercial models. While I acknowledge that there are considerable differences between many commercial organizations and markets and those in education, it is worth examining the changes which have occurred to see if there are any lessons to be learnt.

In this chapter I will look at some of the trends which have arisen in e-business and e-commerce (the former refers to business to business transactions and the latter to business to customer ones). Obviously there are whole books devoted to such topics, with the danger that they are obsolete the moment they are published, so I have been very selective. The issues raised here are the ones I think will have a long-term effect and are most applicable to education.

Deconstruction

Any organization can be viewed as a collection of units performing a variety of functions. In a typical commercial organization you might have departments for sales, production, accounts, and so on. Put simplistically, when it is more economically viable to have these functions grouped together, then an organization is formed. There are benefits in having the sales team working with the production team as part of the same company. Much of the reason why there is an economic advantage in grouping different functions together under one organizational umbrella lies with the benefits of having them physically co-located. If the organization needs a building, then it is better in terms of cost and communication to have everyone in the same building than many separate ones.

The Net begins to alter some of these economic assumptions. When an organization becomes an online entity, each of its functions can be subject to competition. As we saw in the last chapter the removal of costly overheads, while maintaining the communication benefits, leads to the arrival of new competitors. In such a scenario the economical viability of grouping all the functions in one organization is undermined. Many of the tasks the organization needs to perform may now be handled more cost effectively by outsourcing them. The organization is then free to concentrate on the part of the business it does best, be it manufacturing a certain product, retailing clothes or whatever.

Again, there is nothing particularly new about this. Companies have been outsourcing with abandon over the past few years. It is not always successful either, since an organization is more than the sum of its functions. It is a social entity also, and much of the way an organization operates is embedded in the informal interactions that take place in this social context. But if we leave aside whether it is always beneficial to adopt this approach, the point here is whether the Net makes it more likely to occur. As I have mentioned, the Net alters some of the basic economic relationships that existed previously. It also increases the breadth of competition available for any particular function, for example by making it possible for organizations realistically to outsource to consultants in other countries.

One can see how this might have a serious impact upon education and the nature of universities. A university can be viewed as a collection of functions united on one campus. Noam (1995) suggested three main activities, which can be labelled research, library and teaching. To these one could add accreditation, administration and social function. If the deconstruction view is correct, each of these could be performed for less cost by external consultants. Oblinger (2001) applies a business model to education and suggests it can be viewed as a 'value chain':

One way to conceptualize this educational value chain is to think of the interrelationship of the following activities: curriculum development;

content development; learner acquisition and support; learning delivery; assessment and advising; articulation; and credentialling.

Historically, higher education institutions have provided this entire value chain for students. Today there are a number of new entrants to education who might provide some of these services.

In such a system online libraries might charge a one-off fee to students for the use of their services, but the students are not affiliated with any one university. Teaching is performed by a mixture of freelance tutors and access to online content, for example from a publisher. Research is performed in conjunction with industry or funding bodies, carried out by freelance researchers whose affinity is with a global network of researchers in that field. A separate organization offers accreditation for a fee, assessing the courses students have taken and compiling them into a cohesive degree.

This is a very distributed network that loosely associates into an educational system. In the previous chapter I argued that the campus university was unlikely to disappear completely because it still fulfilled a role for a set of students, although there would be a growing proportion who would realize their education through other means. The deconstruction view is a continuation of this argument, one that sees a fundamental shift in society and employment. The extreme view of this sees people no longer employed by a company, but each of us as self-employed consultants whose allegiance is not to any organization, but to a distributed network of associates. The Net has seen a great many people setting up as individual consultants, and this is likely to continue. However, organizations offer a number of benefits that can only be realized for large numbers of people. These include the social function mentioned previously, but also incentives such as health care, pensions, childcare, as well as job security. Such incentives are increasingly significant when employees choose the company they wish to work for, and by making a virtue of such benefits, the organization maintains its status.

There is a convenience for students, employers and employees in maintaining the university system, so it is unlikely to collapse completely. However, increased fragmentation will occur as a result of the Net, and the notion of what constitutes an undergraduate education will become much more diverse than it is currently.

Affiliation and cooperation

There was much excitement a few years ago about affiliation as a new economic model made realizable by the technology. It works through a Web site signing up other sites to act as affiliates. The affiliates recommend people to the original site, and the original site owner pays them a commission on every sale that ensues. So, for example, a site about Jane Austen might have links to an online bookstore, saying, 'Buy *Pride and Prejudice* at Amazon.' If the user follows that link, then

Amazon can track where they have come from, and pays a commission to the Jane Austen site on any books the user purchases on that visit. Although still used widely, particularly in search engines, the affiliate idea became overworked and did not always represent a sound economic model either for the referrer (which lost people because they left to go to the other site) or the commissioning site (which was operating on such small margins that the commission meant they were losing money on some sales).

There are obvious ways in which affiliation could be introduced in education, and this is a very real example of the commercialization of education. Instead of sending students to a bookshop in town which makes all the profit, an online course can recommend students to a particular online bookstore and earn commission on those sales. If the online bookstore is as cheap as other alternatives, one might argue this is simply a good way of the university earning some money which previously had all gone to the bookstores. But it raises many concerns and suspicions. Is the recommended site the best one for students or the one offering the best commission rates? Would the choice of set text be influenced by the deals available? What happens to the money that is gained this way (for instance, there might be less resistance if it went directly to the student's union than if it went to pay managerial bonuses)? Instead of gaining commission for the university, could these savings not be passed directly to the students? Affiliation will be one of the first areas where these issues surrounding commercialization are encountered, because it is so easy to implement.

Affiliation is just the most obvious commercial realization of a broader trend that the Net enables, which is collaboration through partnerships and cooperation between organizations. This can be achieved by combining complementary functions, such as the specific expertise of a local agent and the trust and commercial clout of a large organization. For example a local tour operator can link with a major hotel chain to combine their services. This model can also be used to increase the power of smaller organizations. This can be through the creation of buying cartels, so small independent shops, for example, can group together via the Net in order to buy cheaper goods. Or Web based companies can come together to offer a more comprehensive service than any one can offer alone: for example, the restaurants, hotels, bars and tourist attractions in a specific resort might pool all their efforts into one overall Web site for the resort, so that visitors can make all the arrangements before they arrive. The Net also facilitates cooperation in complex tasks such as product design, which might involve the skills of different partners in separate countries.

In education this opportunity to form new networks and arrangements could be very beneficial for many universities. Smaller colleges and universities which are unable to offer some courses to make a complete programme in a subject might make agreements to take the online offerings of another university, thereby expanding the range of degrees they can offer. The students might study all online, or they might study the courses offered by the first university in a face to face context, and the courses from the second university online. Such agreements may be reciprocal, so universities with specialities in some areas and weaknesses in others can create mutually beneficial arrangements, or they can simply be commercial arrangements on a per student basis. Similarly, universities can collaborate on the creation of new joint courses, by pooling expertise. Such arrangements remove the need for every university to have expertise in every area, while allowing them to offer a broad range of courses to meet the needs of students.

Intermediaries

Intermediaries are agents who act between the buyers and sellers in a transaction. Obvious examples of intermediaries include estate agents, stockbrokers and financial advisers. However, the concept can be broadened out to include all parties who are in the middle of a transaction chain. In this way most retailers become intermediaries, since they act between the consumer and the producer of the goods.

The reason this is a viable economic model is that it used not to be feasible for a manufacturer to reach all customers, and the retailer offers convenience by grouping different products in one physical space. Take a car manufacturer, for instance. It would generally not be practicable for it to provide the service of selling cars to an entire country, hence the sales of cars is handled by local dealerships, who are acting as intermediaries. The car dealer also offers other services including financing, servicing and used car sales.

The Net is leading to a process sometimes called disintermediation: that is, the removal of intermediaries from a transaction. Through firms such as E★Trade and Charles Schwab, online stock brokering became one of the first areas to see a dramatic shift in the role of the intermediary. Instead of paying a broker to perform the transactions, individuals could do it directly via the Net. When customers were enabled to create portfolios that tracked stocks and gave them access to relevant news, much of the advisory role of the broker was removed. Similarly, car manufacturers are now selling direct to consumers, although they currently have the uneasy situation of having to maintain good relationships with their dealers also. The additional services the car dealer offers can quickly be located on the Net, so its convenience factor is weakened. The car manufacturer can sell to a broad customer base because much of the transaction can be automated. The consumer can view the alternatives, select the model, colour and accessories, then book delivery and arrange finance and servicing with other online providers at the same time. Once the order is confirmed, the delivery schedule is arranged automatically via the company's internal network. All this can be done without the intervention of a person, making it possible to sell cars to an entire country from one central point.

The Net is thus removing, or at least altering the roles of, many intermediaries. Perhaps more interesting, though, is the creation of new types of intermediaries. The most obvious of these are search engines and portals. These companies act as intermediaries between users and the information they are seeking. They help the user find that information, while selling advertising and other services. With the growth in the quantity of available information and the increasing variety of options, the role of intermediaries who can locate the required service or information or locate the best deal will become increasingly important. Thus there are Web sites that will offer price comparisons of products, others that will find and bid for items in online auctions on your behalf, and yet others run by consumers that offer advice about any service, from hospitals to ISPs (Internet service providers).

Kalakota and Whinston (1996: 21) claim that 'intermediaries comprize a significant proportion of the online economy'. As more education shifts to online provision it is likely the importance of intermediaries will increase here also. There are a number of portals in existence offering advice on where to study, which courses are available online, the cost of various study programmes, user comments on their quality and so forth (although the caveat should be added here that the portal business model in e-commerce is one that has not always worked as well as anticipated). With the diversity of study the Net offers, such intermediaries will play an important role in helping students select the appropriate course. Offering students a good educational experience becomes even more important in such a scenario, because they will be quick to disseminate views on a course or university, which can be read by prospective students. This is the power of the Net – unlike the carefully chosen quotes for a university prospectus, students can find out what previous students really thought. This makes a good reputation in teaching a valuable commodity. Many universities and colleges that have good teaching quality, but whose reputation is lessened through not being a recognized research institution, may find that this redresses the balance somewhat.

The online educator may have allegiance with more than one institution, delivering different courses for two or three institutions and performing research for another, all of which are geographically remote from their actual location (where he or she might teach a face to face course). Such arrangements blur the boundaries of what constitutes an organization and an employer. In this case universities take on an intermediary role between the freelance academic and the student.

Disintermediation in education will arise if the deconstruction of the education system outlined above takes place. In this view the university ceases to act as an intermediary between the student and the educator. If the system becomes deconstructed, then students and educators could form their own contracts without the need for an intermediary (or without the need for an intermediary in the current form). This would require substantial social change, both in the ways in which education is performed, and in how it is recognized (both officially in terms of accreditation, and in the broader sense within society and employment, since a degree could no longer be said to come from one single university). So there is still a convenience factor for both students and educators in working with the intermediary, but the justification for this is not as strong once the benefits of physical colocation are removed.

The disintermediation and new intermediary scenarios see a dramatic shift in the role of the university. One can already view the university as an intermediary – it brings academics together to work on related research, it acts between students requiring an education and those who provide it, and it provides the different resources required for these functions. This intermediary function has arisen mainly (although the need for accreditation and quality control is also a dominant factor) as a product of the need to be colocated in the same physical space. If this constraint is removed, then it is likely that the nature of the intermediary role it gave rise to will alter also. Given the paradoxical nature of the Net, it is not unreasonable to expect both the new intermediary role and the disintermediation scenario to be realized.

Richness and reach

Evans and Wurster (2000) propose that with regard to transactions, there has always been a trade-off between the richness and the reach of information. Richness is the quality of the experience in terms of the bandwidth or amount of information, the degree of customization, the interactivity it allows, the reliability of the information, its security and its currency, or up-to-dateness. Reach is the number of people who can participate in the sharing of that information. If we take a simple example, a mail order catalogue has a large reach since many people can access it, but low richness, since it is not customizable, or interactive, is usually low in quantity of information and so on. A specialist shop on the other hand is high in richness since such shops are usually staffed by knowledgeable people who will offer helpful advice suited to your particular needs. It is thus customizable, interactive, current, high in bandwidth and reliable. It is low on reach, however, since there is only one shop, and the assistant can only interact with one customer at a time. Chain stores are somewhere in the middle since they have a larger reach than the single specialist shop, but this larger reach means the staff are not as knowledgeable or the experience as rich as with the specialist shop; however, it is richer than for the mail order catalogue. The richness versus reach trade-off is shown in Figure 3.1.

Evans and Wurster contest that the Internet means this trade-off no longer applies – you can have both richness and reach. For example, an online bookstore can offer customization through individual recommendations, it is more up to date than any printed information can be, it is interactive (for instance, you can refine recommendations, join discussion forums, contribute reviews, etc), reliable and so forth. It also has tremendous reach since it can be accessed by different people in different locations simultaneously. It is this ability to add both richness and reach which makes the Internet such a potentially powerful tool for commerce.

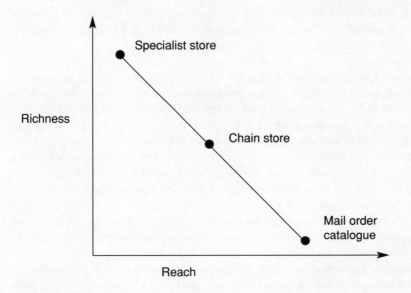

Figure 3.1   *The trade-off between richness and reach*

Source: Evans and Wurster, 2000

In education, the ability to increase the reach of any institution is what, so far, has attracted the most attention. Many universities now feel they can reach new students, by offering courses at a distance, or that they can increase the number of students on existing courses without additional cost. While this may be of interest to the managers of universities, it does not offer much in terms of interest or benefit for the educators themselves. This may be why some online education programs have met with resistance, because they seem to be about gaining more without any investment.

However, if one looks at the Net as a means of improving both reach and richness, then it begins to offer more for educators. Compared with traditional distance education, the obvious means of adding richness is through some form of computer conferencing. This instantly adds a dimension of interactivity to the course, as students can now engage with each other and the educator on a much more frequent basis than was possible before. This needs to be structured properly, however: simply adding a conference to an existing course will bring some rewards for students, but in order to gain the full benefits it needs to be integrated into the course. I will return to this in Chapter 6.

The possibility of adding richness compared with distance education is perhaps more apparent than when compared with face to face education. Surely the face to face situation cannot be beaten for richness? This is one of the reasons why educators need to rethink their approach when using the Net. Simply repeating the same pedagogy as in face to face does not add richness. However, consider an online course which:

● contains different media, for example video clips of the prominent people in the field, audio of a related drama production or reading, animations to bring a process to life, interactive quizzes to test understanding, etc;
● has structured discussion which takes place over an extended period, giving students time to participate and think about the issues;
● makes use of a wide range of resources such as different articles, access to a database of primary resources, recorded discussion of a particular debate, etc;
● is well supported so students can ask questions and receive responses in a reasonable time-frame;
● incorporates real-time events such as an online lecture from an eminent person in the field, with questions afterwards. Such events are easier to organize if the speaker does not have to be physically present;
● provides a customizable environment which students can personalize so information they are interested in is delivered to their desktop: for example, announcements of publications in a certain journal, course information, updates from a social club they belong to.

Such a course adds a degree of richness that begins to look more attractive than many lecture courses.

Clicks and mortar

The so-called 'clicks and mortar' approach creates a mutually beneficial relationship between the physical presence many existing companies have and their online outlets. After the initial excitement about totally online companies had subsided in 2000, a combined approach, which utilized both the advantages of the Net and the physical assets of companies, was seen as the best economic model. This combination can work in a company's favour in several ways. First, they have an established name, and as I mentioned in the previous chapter, a recognizable brand is important in the online environment. Many new online companies spend vast sums of money on advertising because they need to establish such a name and online presence. The physical presence of shops in high streets and shopping malls performs this task for many retailers. This creates a brand that consumers both know and trust. In an article entitled 'Smart business 50' in ZDNet.com, 17 October 2000, the technology officer at Staples.com commented, 'It's like we're running in a marathon and someone gave us a ride in a car for the first half of the race.' Second, the existing company has an established set of operations, for example the storing of goods, customer service and finances.

For this reason, online grocery shopping did not become the domain of a new, online company, but rather it became another outlet for existing supermarket chains. These have the stock and, through their nationwide supermarkets outlets, a ready-made delivery network for online shopping.

Perhaps the most significant combination is in the use of the different modes to complement each other. For instance, if shopping can be delivered easily at home, then those who choose actually to go shopping may want it to be more of a pleasurable experience. We have already seen the number of cafés and restaurants in supermarkets increasing. This could be extended so that customers order online and then go to the store, where they may do some more shopping for items that are difficult to buy online, have a meal, and then collect their packaged shopping on the way out. Another approach is to integrate the online presence in the store, for example by adding a bank of computers with access to the store's Web site. This expands the inventory the store can hold and also takes advantage of the face to face support offered in a store, so a member of staff can help the customer with queries about online products. This places helpful, friendly customer service as a positive benefit over the online experience, so its value is raised in the company.

The clicks and mortar approach has obvious parallels in education, as universities are in the same position as existing retailers – they have a large physical presence which has previously been the focus of their efforts. This can be an encumbrance for some of the reasons I covered in the previous chapter. The solely online organization can operate with fewer constraints and costs and without many of the legacies found in existing organizations. However, if it is part of an overall strategy, the physical presence of an existing organization can be made into an advantage. This is the position most universities currently find themselves in. As the quote above emphasizes, the existing structures can provide a head start in this area, but this will only happen if a deliberate strategy to utilize this advantage is employed. In the fast moving world of the Net, such an advantage can easily be lost.

Boom and bust

The e-commerce boom saw many Web based companies with exaggerated stock market prices and often no discernible business plan. At one time Yahoo's stock was greater than that of Boeing, and famously Amazon's stock pricing exceeded the combined efforts of Barnes and Noble, K-Mart and J C Penney. Small Web sites set up for fun were floated on the stock exchange for millions of pounds, as people rushed to gain some foothold in the new economy. Clearly something had to give, and in the second half of 2000 it did, with the collapse of high-profile online companies such as boo.com and billions of pounds lost in the stock evaluation of e-commerce companies (the stock market valuation of just three companies – Amazon, AOL and Yahoo – went down by some £200 billion from their pricing at the peak of the boom). This was largely inevitable since the boom was based on unrealistic predictions and many companies simply failed to have a viable business model. What the bust also demonstrates, however, is that establishing a successful online operation is not easy. It is not simply a matter of setting up a Web site and waiting for the money to roll in. In order to establish a viable online operation there needs to be a robust logistical network in place, a brand name needs to be established, and there needs to be a real market for the product or service. Establishing these takes time and, importantly, a good deal of money. The idea that an online operation can be a cheap alternative has quickly lost credibility.

There is good news and bad news for education here. The good news is that many of the gloomy predictions about the death of universities that we saw in the last chapter are based on the assumption that an online company can operate at significantly lower cost. While this may be true in the long term, much of the evidence from the e-commerce market seems to suggest that new entrants have significant start-up costs which may put them at an initial disadvantage (for instance in marketing so as to establish an online brand). Having an established name and set of operations gives existing universities a possible advantage, as we saw in the previous section. The bad news is that developing an online offering is not going to be the cheap option many university managers envisage it to be. It is unlikely to be something which can be done 'on the side' as it were. It will require significant investment, in terms of technology, promotion and most importantly in staff. Developing a good online offering is not something staff can do while maintaining current workloads, so they will need to be bought out from these or new staff brought in for the online provision. For many universities with limited resources, such costs may prove prohibitive, which will mean they lose the advantage they currently possess.

Lessons for implementation

Now we have examined, albeit briefly, some of the pertinent issues in e-commerce, there are some lessons that can be applied to education. These are applicable both to an individual educator and the overall organization.

I Add both richness and reach

Good online organizations add both richness and reach to their offerings, not just one or the other. There is a lesson here for educational establishments. Currently too many envisage the Net as a means of adding reach, but with distinctly less richness. The streaming lecture approach is an example of this. It increases reach in that the number of students who can receive the lecture is greatly improved. This allows the university to reach students they could not have previously, for example those geographically remote from the campus, or those with time commitments that prevent full-time, face to face study. This is without the need for new buildings or even new staff. Increasing reach is important, and can be a positive move in education as it brings people into an educational environment who otherwise might be excluded. It is not, however, sufficient for successful online education. A course which focuses purely on increasing reach offers a less rich experience than the face to face one, for the reasons I highlighted in Chapter 3. Some will argue that you can never make the online experience richer than the face to face one, but the effort should certainly be made to add different forms of richness. Merely using the Net to increase the reach of the institution posits the distance or online student as a poor relation to the campus based one.

2   Decide upon a strategy regarding face to face and online implementation

Both at the individual course and the overall university level it is important to decide upon a strategy with regard to the Net. Such a strategy may be not to go online at all, but even such a decision has the result that a virtue is made of the face to face approach. This places an emphasis on making this approach a positive alternative to online study, with a potential reworking of how that methodology is implemented. As suggested at the end of the last chapter, such an approach also means the university makes a virtue of the benefits associated with its physical presence. This not only offers a means of fighting competition from the new entrants in the market, but it also forces a reappraisal of the value of teaching. Another option is to adopt a hybrid approach (again either across the university or on a particular course) along the lines suggested in the previous chapter. The other end of the continuum is a fully online course or university. Some universities will choose to set this up as a separate entity, while others will do it within the existing organizational framework.

The key, though, is to think through the implications for the university or the course and to decide upon a strategy, which can be supported and backed up. Merely leaving matters to take their own path is unlikely to lead to a satisfactory outcome.

3   Be aware of new roles and working practices

The Net will change the nature of organizations, including universities, and the nature of working patterns. The initial hype in the 1990s surrounding tele-working subsided, but now many people find themselves working more and more at home. As the bandwidth and the enabling tools for this expand, this option will increase. The provision of online courses will speed things further. On both the individual and organizational level it is important to appreciate these changes and be able to adapt to them. A university may find itself employing more part-time academics who are remote from the campus, or taking on a role as a local education portal. Academics may find they create new networks and associations, and their skills can be better employed teaching separate courses they are comfortable with, rather than being forced to teach subjects as part of an overall curriculum.

4   Use the Net to develop a network of partners and contacts

As I discussed in the previous chapter, the Net is already facilitating the establishment of new networks between researchers. Mailing lists, discussion conferences and collective Web sites have all helped researchers foster new relationships with other specialists beyond the scope of their own university. There has always been a tradition of this, through conferences, joint research projects and the like, but the Net makes it easier and broadens the possible contacts. The same networks are now beginning to be created for the other branch of academic function, teaching. Often teaching is viewed as something of a poor cousin to research. It is the eminent researchers who tend to get promoted and who are well known names at a university. By creating communities of good practice, the Net may be a means of raising the profile of the teaching role. For universities it offers a means of strengthening their curriculum through teaching partnerships.

5   Take advantage of existing practices

Universities are currently in the position many of the incumbent retailers found themselves in back in 1998. There is a threat from new online providers which can offer potential benefits and cost reduction to the existing organizations. By utilizing the advantages of their existing name, structures and processes the incumbents can gain a distinct advantage over new entrants at this early stage. However, the pace of change is rapid, and vacillation could see this advantage being squandered.

6   Be prepared to invest

The online provision of courses that add both richness and reach is something that will require investment in terms of time, people and finances. It is unlikely to reap immediate benefits since it requires new methods and systems to be developed and adapted. There is always an upfront cost in doing this, so the first few courses are likely to take an excessive amount of time and energy to realize and support. This will lead to systems for dealing efficiently with the demands of online education, but both educators and managers need to be aware that it is likely to take time to accomplish and will not offer a quick solution.

Conclusion

In this chapter I have examined some of the themes from the e-commerce arena that might have a bearing in the educational one. There are undoubtedly different constraints and issues in the two areas, and not all of the trends that have been observed in the commercial sector will have their counterpart in education. However, the Net is ideal for selling information goods, which rely on discourse, text, images, and the like. Education is an ideal market for the Net, since many of its functions can be transferred and even enriched in an online environment. It also has a knowledgeable audience that is keen to use the technology (this does not apply to all areas of education, but will become increasingly the case as current school children enter higher education). The commercial pressure on education is only going to increase, so it is sensible to see what lessons can be learnt from commercial operations.

Many universities are currently offering online courses, for a variety of reasons. In the next chapter I will look at these reasons.

Summary

This chapter examined the following issues in e-commerce, and how they might have a similar effect in education:

- deconstruction;
- affiliation and cooperation;
- intermediaries and disintermediation;
- richness and reach;
- clicks and mortar;
- the reasons behind the e-commerce boom and bust.

Six lessons from implementation were suggested:

- Add both richness and reach.
- Decide upon a strategy regarding face to face and online implementation.
- Be aware of new roles and working practices.
- Use the Net to develop a network of partners and contacts.
- Take advantage of existing practices.
- Be prepared to invest.

Chapter 4

Motivations for adopting the Net

Introduction

So far in this book I have stressed the reasons why the Net has potential as an educational technology, and some of the broader issues surrounding the Net and education. It is of course already in use in a great range of courses and in a variety of roles. In this chapter we will look at the current situation, and some of the reasons educators or institutions have for using the Net.

Much of this chapter has been derived from my experiences of attending numerous presentations detailing how the Net is being used on one course or another. The content of educational technology conferences saw a dramatic change in the 1990s. In the early 1990s there was a preponderance of papers detailing the use of multi-media, but by 1999 these had seemingly all disappeared, and almost every presentation was now on the use of the Net. This reinforces an earlier point about the enthusiasm and often false optimism people hold out for educational technologies. It also demonstrates the rapid rate of change in the field, and the disruptive nature of the Net.

What follows are some broad categories of what can be generally termed 'motivations' for adopting the Net. It is sometimes difficult to discern an original motivation from an unpredicted outcome – everyone indulges in *post hoc* rationalization, but it is often the case that, swept away by enthusiasm, we do not stop before embarking on a project and ask the fundamental question, 'Why are we doing this?'

Educator enthusiasm

A factor that is often sufficient for a course to adopt a Net-based approach is enthusiasm for these technologies on the part of the educator. The Net tends to have this effect on people: they get 'bitten by the bug' on an individual basis, and the question becomes one of 'How can I incorporate this into my course?'

The adoption of the Net in teaching follows many of the traditional patterns of technology penetration, or institutional change. An S-shaped curve of diffusion of innovation is seen in many organizations (Rogers, 1995), with the number of adopters increasing over time. So early on there is a relatively small group of pioneers, and 'early adopters' in organizations, who tend to recognize the potential of new ideas, will embrace new technology, and are keen to implement it. Such pioneers are often enthusiastic about a technology beyond its current capabilities – in Christensen's terms it is disruptive and currently offers less than traditional methods. Crucially, however, it has some features that appeal to these early pioneers. For example, when CMC (computer mediated communication) was still relatively new, and the software often unreliable and difficult to use, there was a strong community of people in education who were devotees of it. Many will still recall these days with a sense of nostalgia.

In the OU for instance, use of CMC on courses dates back to 1988. The conferencing software used then was known as CoSy, and it relied on a text-based interface (as opposed to a graphical one driven by a mouse). It had a number of good features, but was not particularly intuitive to use. It required a certain level of investment on the part of the user to employ effectively, which meant it attracted students and academics with an enthusiasm for the technology. Many recall the sense of community that existed in those early CMC days. In an evaluation of early CMC implementation, Robin Mason and Paul Bacsich (1998: 250) state, 'the level of input from tutors with successful conferences usually far exceeds the number of hours for which they are paid. Many tutors have been prepared to put in "unpaid" hours because the medium is novel and they are curious and enthusiastic.' This is still an issue with online tutoring today. They also report on a central academic who spent 10 hours a week in maintaining a small-population online course. The OU has always operated on economies of scale, so for a central academic (as opposed to a part-time tutor) to be expending so much time in presentation means the approach is not scalable. We shall return to these issues of presentation costs in a later chapter.

After the early adopters there is a middle group who have a pragmatic attitude to the technology. If it becomes easy enough to use and offers significant gains, then they will adopt it. This group represents how most people approach technology in everyday use. When the mobile phone became cheap enough, easy to use, and truly mobile, then it became a viable technology for most people. The same can be seen with the adoption of PCs and the Internet. With CMC in the OU it quickly moved from one or two courses in the late 1990s to 20,000 students in 1996 and now over 140,000. This large-scale take-up occurred when the technology became more reliable and easier to use, so both students and academics could incorporate it easily into their courses, without it becoming the main focus of study. It also mirrored the take-up of Internet access and e-mail use in the general population. This group of pragmatists probably represents the middle area of the normal distribution curve, which is by definition where the majority of people are situated. One of the implications of this is that once uptake of a technology moves beyond the early adopters and reaches the middle group, the number of users increases rapidly.

There are then those who are resistant to change. When that change is brought on by technology, the technophobic will be a strong group in this resistance. We have already encountered some of the arguments against the use of the Net in Chapter 2. Although often presented as concerns about the quality of education, what underlies much resistance is a fear about the potential of the technology to alter one's personal situation. Will it ultimately mean one's status, or even job, is threatened? Is the technology in conflict with some deeply held value? Will it mean learning a new way of working? I have found myself occasionally in heated arguments which on the surface seem to be about trivial matters, such as the preference of one software package over another, but in fact they are more about deeply held, and often opposing, values. The difficulty in such cases is identifying what it is you are disagreeing over in the first place.

In the early stages of developing T171 there was a great deal of debate about the role of the Web browser and conferencing software in the course. On the surface this seemed to be about preferences over software, but we came to appreciate that in fact it was about what we felt was the most effective teaching method. The proponents of the conferencing software saw dialogue and discussion as the key element, and viewed the browser as a means of simply delivering information. The browser camp viewed the Web and particularly the browser as the interface through which students would perform all of their online functions (this was back in 1998 when the browser had not quite reached the penetration it has now). Of course, both camps were right, and having established what the debate was really about we could develop a solution that was satisfactory to both. In this case it involved making the Web site the central component of the course and allowing access to the conferencing software through both the Web interface and the client, and making dialogue and group work a key element of the course approach.

At this stage of Net use in education, many of the educators who have used it extensively are early adopters, and therefore likely to be enthusiastic and willing to devote extra time and energy to its use. Its uptake is now reaching the middle group of pragmatists, which suggests that the number of online courses is set to increase exponentially over the next few years. In an investigation of the take-up of the Web in teaching in 1999, Ferrarini and Poindexter found that lack of university incentive was not a significant factor in its implementation. Educators were implementing it out of personal, rather than institutional motivation at this

stage. This is the way c   ...ns – it comes from the
bottom up rather than fi

This was seen with th   ...on of personal computers in companies.
When the Apple II compu   ...s on the market in the early 1980s, its 'killer app'
(the piece of software that made it invaluable) was a spreadsheet called VisiCalc.
This was in the days before Excel and Lotus 1-2-3, and VisiCalc was the first
spreadsheet available. It was a boon to middle management, who could now do all
manner of projections with figures and ask 'what-if' questions, such as 'What if
we raise the price of each item by 1 cent, and buy two more production
machines?' The top-level management in most large companies were not interested in actually using computers; they had IT specialists with expensive IBM
mainframes who performed such tasks. And those mainframe specialists were not
interested in buying the little Apple II computers. Meanwhile, the middle
managers could never get access to the mainframes to play around with and ask
the sort of questions they wanted to ask. At around $2,000, however, they could
buy an Apple II out of their own budgets, so without organizations realizing it,
and certainly without its being a senior management directive, PCs became a
significant part of the organization.

This 'infiltration by stealth' process is what happened initially in many educational establishments with regard to the Net, with enthusiasts putting up 'home
made' Web sites. Now, as the technology shifts to the middle group and becomes
accepted, most universities have an official stance on its use, and a significant Web
presence. However, at this transition phase, its implementation in courses is still
occurring on an ad hoc basis in many institutions, with the drive and enthusiasm
of individual educators being the main reason for take-up.

While inevitable, this pattern of uptake is not without its problems. Pioneers
and early adopters are naturally very enthusiastic about the technology. This has
several implications. First, it means their judgement may be clouded somewhat as
to what represents a good use of the technology. They tend to see it as the
panacea for all ills, and set about implementing it in places or with people where
it may not be appropriate (particularly in the early phases of a technology).
Another implication is that it actually makes evaluation of the effectiveness of the
technology problematic. The use of the technology in itself reawakens enthusiasm
in the topic for the educator. If someone has been teaching a course on the same
topic in the same manner for 10 years, and then he or she discovers the Net, and
becomes very enthusiastic about its use, then it is difficult to say whether any
improvement in learning or satisfaction was down to the technology or simply a
by-product of the educator regaining enthusiasm in the topic. This is related to
the novelty effect seen in many reports: that is when both students and teachers
are intrigued by the novelty of the approach, but this effect may wear off in later
years.

Another potential problem arising from the enthusiasm of the early adopters is
that they do not represent a typical or sustainable model. This issue of applying
what the enthusiasts do to a more general population is an important one. If the

model is only sustainable if someone is prepared to devote huge amounts of time and energy to it, then it will not be taken up elsewhere. I have heard cases of such enthusiasts working online until 2.30 every night dealing with queries. Such excessive demands are not scalable if Net technology is to become integrated into the majority of courses, so caution must be taken in evaluating the success of such early courses.

To supplement face to face teaching

Many campus based universities use the Net not to replace their traditional face to face mode of delivery, but rather as a means of supplementing it. This can take different forms: for example, Web pages can be used to provide additional information, or e-mail be used as a means of contacting tutors of large courses. For example, Baiocchi *et al* (1999: 47) relate how a large-scale introductory technology course was supplemented by Web based material: 'The syllabus, topical outline, links to multi-media resources, and access to course instructors via e-mail were additions to the in-class course intended to enrich its potential. Students were still expected to attend class.'

This situates the Net firmly as a sustaining technology, and in this role it offers a number of benefits. Students on campus can use it to access recommended reading or as a means of contacting lecturers, bulletin boards can be used to communicate with students on the same course, and administrative information can be made readily available. Some universities take the notion of providing support material a little further, by using the Web as a means of allowing students to revisit lectures, so they can view a streaming video of the lecture and look at lecture notes. This has benefit in allowing students to take notes at their own pace, and as a resource for revision.

For example, Latchman, Kim and Tingling (1999) use streaming technology to provide students with 'lectures on demand'. These are videos of the actual lecture, combined with lecture notes and e-mail contact. Whereas the first approach was supplementary to lectures, this model can come to replace the lectures for students. Although it is intended as a revision and note-taking aid, it is not difficult to envisage students feeling they do not need to attend lectures because they can always catch them later on the Web. This begins then to sound very similar to the video lecture approach I have mentioned several times already, and is fraught with the same problems. Although on campus, a student who operates in this manner effectively becomes a distance education student. This approach essentially duplicates the pedagogical approach of the face to face presentation, with no concession to the distance aspects of the learner. This is one of the perils of viewing the Net simply as a sustaining technology, in that educators do not re-address their teaching methodology with this view – the technology is a means of adding some value or alleviating some burden from their current tasks. However, this may ignore the actual context in which students interact with the medium.

The medium is the message

There are some courses that deal specifically with the use of the Net, either in its relation to a specific domain such as teaching or health, or in terms of the technology. For such courses the use of the Net is an integral part of the course approach, and students both expect, and want, to engage in using it. As with educator enthusiasm, this is usually one of the first driving factors in the adoption of any technology. For instance, the first courses in the OU to use CMC extensively were an 'Introduction to Information Technology' course, and a course for teachers wanting to learn about computer conferencing. For such courses, using the technology effectively forms an integral part of the academic content of the course.

Similarly, when we developed T171 the content of the course was concerned with using, understanding and appreciating the significance of computers and the Internet. The course is delivered through the Web, with extensive use of computer conferencing. Students produce their assignments in HTML, and work on group activities finding and sharing information on the Web. The use of the Net is then an integral part of the course material; the medium in this case suits the message.

If any educational technology is to become integrated successfully, then it needs to have wider possibilities than in courses about the technology itself. A course on Shakespeare or quantum physics cannot spend a good proportion of its core material teaching students how to use the technology. A certain level of competence has to be assumed for such courses to operate successfully. This has happened with CMC, where the technology has become sufficiently easy to use that it can be accommodated into a wide range of courses not related to the technology. A similar process is now in progress with the use of the Web.

Pedagogic suitability

Other courses have adopted the use of Net technology not because the course is itself about the technology, but rather because the underlying pedagogy of the course suits online delivery. An obvious example of this is in resource based learning, where students can be presented with a wide range of resources, often external to the university. Students derive their own learning experience from these resources within the overall framework of the course. I shall examine this further when we look at pedagogical approaches in the next chapter.

Another popular approach in online courses is that of collaborative or cooperative group work. These have long been favoured approaches in face to face education, and there is evidence that they promote deeper learning and critical thinking (Johnson and Johnson, 1986; Gokhale, 1995). Until the recent advent of communications technology, such collaborative learning was difficult to achieve in distance education, without the use of face to face settings such as tutorials or residential schools. However, with the introduction of communication technologies, group work and collaboration have become a viable pedagogical approach in distance learning courses. This was one of the first motivations and uses for CMC in distance education. Students who would otherwise work in isolation could now work collaboratively on group tasks. Through the use of both synchronous and asynchronous communication, and shared workspaces such as virtual whiteboards, students can collaborate on the same piece of work remotely. Such tasks can take different forms, and these will be explored further in the following chapter.

For existing distance educators, then, there is a clear pedagogic motivation for introducing an online aspect to a course. For face to face educators, though, it surely represents a backward step to replace actual group interaction with an online equivalent. This may not necessarily be true, since the online version does offer one advantage in that interaction can occur asynchronously, with a record of the interaction being generated automatically. Students may find it difficult to arrange face to face sessions where all of them can be present. By using an e-mail list or a text based conferencing system they can all participate over a given period. There are benefits to adopting a combined model of initial face to face meetings to determine the roles of the students and the focus of the project, which are then followed up with online discussion and delivery of individual elements. Much of the initial negotiation of tasks and roles can be time consuming online and is more efficient when conducted face to face.

Institutional benefit

Universities can benefit from the use of the Net in education, both on campus and in reaching new audiences. A growing number of campus based universities are offering distance education courses via the Net. As we saw in an earlier chapter, the traditional cost of creating a distance education course was often prohibitively high for many universities. These now view the production of an online course as relatively inexpensive compared with the requirements of a traditional distance education market. It allows many campus based universities to offer both modes of presentation for some courses, thus expanding their potential student base: for example, by reaching a specific target group working in a particular sector. This represents a student market they would have been unable to reach otherwise. Many universities and colleges also use the Net to take advantage of their position in the local community, for example, by offering 'taster' courses, which can be studied at a distance. The credit for these courses can then contribute towards a degree, so they hope that potential students can 'test the water', and if they find they like studying, they can sign up for conventional degree programmes or part-time study. The type of hybrid models combining distance and campus–based modes of learning that were outlined earlier can also be a useful means of utilizing resources, since this lowers the numbers of student actually on campus at any one time.

Many traditional universities are taking advantage of the Net to maximize their resources, usually the limited number of staff available for large courses. This can mean foundation-type courses can be presented to large student numbers, often without increasing the number of instructors required. In such cases the course, although delivered on campus with students located at the university, is effectively a distance education one. This raises a number of issues that lecturers have to address. They often have to learn very quickly the distance education principles which have been established for many years in conventional distance education establishments. Many such educators can find themselves thrown in at the deep end – the material they have used effectively for delivering lectures is no longer appropriate.

If, as we saw in Chapter 1, there is supposedly no significant improvement in student learning through the use of new technologies, then one of the driving factors behind its continued implementation may well be the benefit, or at least perceived benefit, for institutions, rather than the actual benefit for students.

Ion and O'Donnell (1996) summarize the perceived (though not necessarily actual) benefits of CAL (computer assisted learning) as:

- reduction of staff/student contact hours;
- improved learning environment;
- improved departmental image.

A similar list could apply to Net-based courses. Interestingly, only one of these really relates to benefits for the student. The last perceived benefit, that of departmental, or university image, should not be overlooked either. As with the rush for every business to become an e-business, so there is a certain kudos and marketability in being able to present yourself as part of the 'e-learning' revolution. This is not to undervalue the importance of image either – the perception of students regarding the community they are joining and the education they are receiving is an important element in how they approach their learning experience. If they feel part of an exciting and interesting development, then the personal investment and involvement in that course may well be higher.

One of the most significant factors in the take-up of the Net as an educational tool will be the resource and impetus universities invest in it. Many see the Net as a way of either making better use of existing resources, or reaching new audiences, both of which have implications for increased profitability. For example, Skillicorn (1996: 471) claims that 'Hypermedia technology provides both an opportunity for universities to provide a better learning experience for their students, and a way to cope with funding reductions. Second-generation hypermedia systems makes it cost-effective to develop and deliver multimedia courseware, while permitting learning to occur within a community.'

This has an element of déjà vu – similar things were promised for multi-media

CAL (as Ion and O'Donnell show). There are possibilities for online courses to offer savings: for instance, courses can be produced by selecting from a range of pre-existing design templates and content templates. This means that an academic author can fairly quickly create a prototype course that is close to the finished product. This certainly represents a saving in time and input from different parties over producing quality print items.

However, it ignores the effort that is still required in actually presenting a course. The underlying assumption here is that once the course is produced it is cheap to present. As I have argued previously, this assumes an information transfer model of education rather than a supported constructive one. The new tools may well facilitate production of courses, but there is a downside too, in that they tend to increase the presentation workload. We shall look at this in more detail in a later chapter on issues of scale.

One should not sneer at increased profitability being a reasonable motivation – universities have to operate in harsh economical environments, with often limited resources. If an online course offers as good, if not better, educational experience for the students, and frees up resources for supporting students, academic time for research, or maintaining libraries for instance, then it is of benefit to all. However, a focus on increased profitability on the part of the institution nearly always underestimates the amount of time and effort required to run an online course that works effectively for students and staff. If the motivation is increased profitability or image alone, with scant concern for the student experience, then such courses may well backfire for the institutions in the long term.

As a delivery mechanism for CAL

Computer based training (CBT) and CAL have been well established for many years now, and saw a particular growth in popularity in the early 1990s with wide acceptance of multi-media CD ROMs. These have been used extensively in both face to face and distance education, often providing additional support to traditional teaching methods. They are particularly well suited for simulations, which allow students to experiment with variables, and influence outcomes which may not be easily achieved in the real world: for example, altering gravity in a physics simulation. However, as I discussed earlier, their impact upon general education practice has not matched the early optimism.

The introduction of the Web has seen something of a revival of interest in CAL. Many courses are using the Web to deliver simulations, visualization aids and interactive tools. Some of the applications of CAL are:

- Manipulation of effects and objects. For example, computer graphic principles can be taught by manipulating various objects, lighting effects, textures, and so forth.
- Visualization of abstract concepts. Some concepts can be difficult to under-

stand in abstract terms, but are made more concrete through visualization sequences that the students can control.

- Testing hypotheses that would be dangerous, expensive or impossible to do otherwise. For example if students are allowed to build simulations of electrical circuits they can create ones which will blow without incurring costs. Or biology students can perform experiments in genetics and protein manipulation that would be difficult if not impossible to achieve in a laboratory.
- Manipulate real laboratory equipment. This is a variation on the use of CAL that allows distance students remote access to actual equipment. This can be very beneficial if students are geographically remote from laboratories, or the equipment is dangerous or expensive.

The same sorts of educational benefits are put forward in favour of these Web-based CAL programs as with 'traditional' CAL: they allow students to experiment, they make learning more active and enjoyable, and they demonstrate certain concepts easily that are difficult to express in print or speech. This raises the question why they seem to be more popular when delivered via the Web than previously. For instance, Graf and Schnaider (1999: 71) claim that 'a real breakthrough in the acceptance of CAL could not be achieved... but in recent years, the computer together with the Internet and the Web have again been discovered as a promising educational environment, and the educational community has again noticed advantages of computer aided education.'

Even if you disagree with this statement, it is interesting that someone should claim that the Net has revitalized interest in CAL. Why should this be so? With limitations of bandwidth, the type of CAL that can be distributed through the Net is often inferior to that which can be distributed on CD ROM. This is again an example of the Net being a disruptive technology. In this case the performance is initially inferior to what you might be able to produce on a CD, yet a number of educators see an advantage in delivering their CAL type material through this medium.

There are several reasons why Net-delivered CAL may prove to be more popular than CD. First, as was mentioned in the first chapter, the Web browser offers a common, familiar interface, which many people feel comfortable with. Delivering CAL through this interface may mean users feel less intimidated by the software, and more inclined to try it. Although the actual interface to the CAL is embedded within the program, so each one can differ, it is housed within a familiar and comfortable environment.

Second, it is easily integrated with other resources and communication, thus making the CAL component seamless with the course content as a whole, rather than separated out as distinct components such as print, CD ROM, video and so on. This may seem a minor point, but it recognizes the manner in which many students actually engage with material. When they come across an instruction in a printed unit to listen to an audiocassette, or do a multi-media activity, there are a proportion of students who will do exactly that. There are also those who will think, 'I'll do that later', and never quite get round to it. Placing all your components within a single environment means students can engage with the CAL at the exact point of relevance in the material, without having to change environments.

Another reason why Net based CAL may have better take-up than CD delivered material is related to the issue raised earlier, of the Net allowing the educator to remain close to the material. Producing multi-media CD ROMs can be a daunting task, and one often feels in order to justify a CD, there needs to be a great deal of multi-media material, a well designed interface, installation procedures and so on; and then the CDs need to be pressed. Although Net delivered CAL does require the educator to learn (or have access to one person who knows) languages such as Java or VRML (Virtual Reality Markup Language), an effective result can be produced from a reasonable acquaintance with these languages. It can then easily be incorporated into other material (such as text and images) the educator has produced, and delivered with less relative effort for the educator. Educators can therefore produce one or two CAL elements in an otherwise straightforward Web site on their own or with minimal input from others, without the need to produce enough multi-media elements to fill a CD ROM.

Lastly, one should not ignore the impression of students. As mentioned above, online courses can help to improve the image of a university or department. Many students have a familiarity with the Web and an expectancy of receiving materials this way. The same CAL program delivered by other means may not have the same impact for such students.

Lessons for implementation

The possible motivations I have looked at here can be summarized crudely as 'Are you creating an online course for personal, student or institutional benefit?' The answer will ideally be all three, since a successful implementation should obviously be for the benefit of students, but should also have the backing of educators and be part of an overall strategy within the university. Looking at this categorization of current reasons behind Net uptake provides some useful suggestions for successful implementation.

I   Start with the enthusiasts

The issue of educator enthusiasm is an essential ingredient, and this represents an issue for organizations. Top-down directives are often problematic in education, and as we saw in Chapter 2 there is considerable resistance to the Internet from many educators. So a command to make a course Net-based is unlikely to be successful if the educator responsible is not enthusiastic about the medium. Enthusiasm is likely to come from certain quarters and individuals, but once these have developed their courses, the organization is faced with the problem of how to foster enthusiasm among other educators if it wants large-scale uptake. One means of achieving this is to make a showcase of successful courses that have been implemented by the early enthusiasts. As the saying goes, nothing succeeds like doing. While many people can provide reasons for not doing something, once it has been implemented successfully these reservations tend to disappear. Seeing a course delivered successfully, with high student demand, creates its own motivation. The enthusiasts can provide valuable lessons for other educators who are perhaps less confident with the technology. In order to do so the pioneers need to be encouraged to run workshops and give presentations, which may mean buying them out from other duties. This dissemination of experience and good practice is common in research, but less so in teaching within universities. It should particularly be encouraged when there is a radical shift in the method of teaching, which online courses represent compared with traditional lecturing.

2   Implement a staff development framework

Another method of fostering enthusiasm for the medium is through careful staff development. For those who are wary of the technology this can start with demonstrating its benefits, and encouraging them to create their own material. Since 1997 I have been involved with different courses that help students create a Web page at some point. More than 30,000 students have done this with the OU, and I have yet to encounter a person who is not delighted when he or she uploads his or her first Web page. The same is true of educators. Once general mistrust of the medium is overcome, the institution then has a role in encouraging educators to see the potential educational benefits, and developing an understanding of how to use the medium effectively.

The current large uptake of the Net as an educational tool raises a number of issues for many educators. As has already been mentioned, and as we shall see in detail in the next chapter, delivering material through the Net often means using a different pedagogical approach from face to face lectures, and even from conventional distance education materials. For instance, writing effectively for the Web has different issues and values from print and requires a different style. The shift to online delivery effectively transforms all educators into distance educators, even if they are using the Net to support face to face teaching, because the students are interacting with the material remotely from the provider, either spatially or temporally. This means any educator wanting to provide online learning material benefits from learning distance education principles about delivery of material, the type of material used, support available, production of material and so on. I have seen too many online courses which profess to be distance education, but are in effect the lecturer's notes saved in HTML format and posted on the Web. This does not constitute a good online course. Students need more detailed material, a clear structure, and interaction with each other and the tutors. At this stage of its uptake the implementation of Net technologies is often performed by one or two interested individuals, and often outside the conventional university structure. Institutions that wish to have an online course presence have a responsibility to provide both technical and pedagogical advice for educators who are developing these courses. Many institutions are beginning to implement structured approaches, usually in terms of technical support, design and delivery. Coherent approaches that combine this with an awareness of the different pedagogical styles required for this medium are still somewhat rare, though.

So as I have argued elsewhere, it is important not to view such courses or technology as existing in isolation. The enthusiastic educator can go a long way to starting the implementation of these technologies, but ultimately the institution has to develop a cohesive plan to foster their uptake.

3   Start with courses where there is an undeniable justification

A question which is often asked is 'When is this approach suitable?' For the sort of courses highlighted above where the medium is the message, or where there is a clear pedagogic advantage, the application is obvious. But what about other courses? In the initial implementation of such courses it is a good idea to combine enthusiastic educators with receptive students. So for the first few such courses, topic areas which have a direct relevance, or where there is a clear benefit, are advantageous since they provide an environment with a willing audience which is keen to engage with the technology and approach and provide feedback. This can be in an obvious area, such as teaching about using the technology effectively in a given domain, but it can also be found in unexpected areas: for example, courses with a minority interest, such as one focusing on a relatively obscure artist, can benefit from bringing together the small worldwide community, and allowing students to participate in this. There is a strong ripple effect, however, and once there are a number of students with experience of working this way, they come to expect similar courses to be offered across the university.

My response to the question of when the Net is applicable, is that it is applicable in almost any domain you care to think of, provided you rethink the material in an appropriate manner. Whether there is a market for such a course is a different issue, but an important one. There are probably some topic areas where the student audience is unlikely to want to use the technology, or does not have access to it, and so no matter how good the course, the students would not sign up for it. I hesitate to suggest any such areas, because whenever I have done so in the past, I have always received strong objections from people saying, 'Not all X students are the same, I love using the Net.' And they are quite right. If the three vectors of educator, institution and students combine in support for a course, then it stands a good chance of success.

Conclusion

The motivations covered here are by no means exhaustive, nor are they exclusive. It is probably rare for just one motivation to be in place: there will usually be a combination of them in play. When you consider using the Net in teaching, you should consider the motivations for its adoption from the outset. Such critical reflection on the reasoning behind the course will raise a number of issues which implementers should address before embarking on course production and releasing material to students. For instance, is the implementation being performed solely because of educator enthusiasm, or for institutional benefit? In either case, one must consider whether it will enhance the learning experience of students. If the institution is primarily concerned with increased profitability, has it realistically assessed the costs of creating a good online course? Has the learning experience for students been thought through?

These motivations are based on what is happening currently. Given the likely increase in Internet access, improvements in bandwidth and general penetration into all areas of society, it may be the case that these motivations will be less significant, or simply will not matter at all. Online education will just happen, almost by default, since being online will be such a part of our everyday lives.

In the next chapter we will begin to look at the issues of implementation in more detail, starting with arguably the most important factor, course pedagogy.

Summary

In this chapter six main motivations for currently adopting the Net in teaching have been identified:

- educator enthusiasm;
- supplementing face to face teaching;
- topic suitability;
- pedagogic suitability;
- institutional benefit;
- as a CAL delivery mechanism.

From these six motivations, three lessons for implementation were drawn:

- Start with enthusiasts.
- Implement a staff development framework.
- Start with courses where there is an undeniable justification.

Chapter 5

Pedagogies for online teaching

Introduction

The previous chapters have focused on the significance of the Net and its broader impact upon education. It is important to consider such issues because the manner in which a technology is implemented is shaped by the beliefs one holds about its role in education and the value it can offer. The remaining chapters of the book will focus more directly on implementation issues. The first, and probably most important, of these is the pedagogical approach adopted by the course.

For many academics pedagogy is not an issue they have had to be concerned with to any great extent. After completing a PhD they simply lectured, often with little practice or advice. Recent developments have seen an emphasis on promoting teaching quality in many countries, so lecturers are encouraged to engage in self-reflection and exchange good practice. When it comes to teaching on the Net, the assumptions implicit in the standard lecture model do not easily map across to the new medium, and in order to create an effective online course many educators are forced to investigate new teaching methods, often for the first time in their careers.

In this chapter some of the approaches that have been adopted on the Net are covered. The amount of space that can be given to topics which elsewhere command whole books is limited, but I hope you can gain a flavour of the approaches and the philosophies underlying them. There is a good deal of overlap between some of the pedagogies outlined, and the categories used here are by no means agreed upon: for instance, I have made collaborative work a separate category to constructivism, where many would argue that the former is merely a way of implementing the latter. There are also degrees to which any one approach might be implemented.

Constructivism

Constructivism is probably the dominant learning approach in online courses. It is heavily influenced by the work of psychologist Jerome Bruner, but has become a broad term to encompass a general approach. It is a learning theory rather than a teaching theory, so it can be realized in terms of teaching in a variety of ways, some of which we cover in this chapter. The philosophy behind constructivism is that learners construct their own knowledge, based on their experience and relationship with concepts. Each learner therefore has a unique representation of the knowledge, formed by constructing his or her own solutions and interpretations to problems and ideas. This carries with it several concomitant notions:

- It emphasizes a social construction of knowledge, so the learner comes to an understanding of a concept through dialogue with other learners and the teacher.
- It gives importance to the context of learning, so approaches which encourage learners to participate in a valid activity such as project or research-based courses are favoured (see also 'Situated learning', page 75).
- Collaborative activities are often placed at the heart of the course, since such activities encourage both of the above (see 'Collaborative learning').
- It shifts the focus of attention from the teacher to the learner. This makes the role of the educator a more facilitative one, rather than the transmitter of knowledge. This has been called a transition to being a 'guide on the side' instead of a 'sage on the stage'.

The reason constructivism seems to be such a popular approach with online courses is that it seems to suit many of the advantages the Net can bring to distance situations. The more didactic pedagogy of face to face lecturing does not translate well onto the Net, and so an approach that places less emphasis on the educator and more on the learner, and that positively encourages communication, seems to offer an alternative that makes the online course a distinct, and perhaps more attractive, offering. Typically, then, a course that adopts some element of constructivism will incorporate structured discussion, group work and possibly an emphasis on interpreting concepts in the light of one's experience.

There are degrees to the extent that such an approach might be adopted. There are many subjects where there is in fact one correct interpretation of a concept and it would be positively dangerous to encourage students to all develop a different understanding. Any form of engineering is such an area. Students need to understand absolutely that materials will crack if put under certain stress or chemicals will behave in a prescribed manner if combined. For most subjects there is probably a core set of such principles. However, students can still create a deeper understanding of such concepts through discussion or activity, rather than simply being told they are the case. Many courses might combine an element of instruction (through text, lecture, animation or some other medium) with an associated activity that encourages students to explore the concepts. Courses which take a more purist constructivist approach will provide a framework for students to discuss issues, with each of them providing their own interpretation, but the educator will always refrain from providing a correct answer. Such an approach can be rewarding, but also frustrating for students.

The constructivist movement has been influential in emphasizing the role of the learner and the individual in education, and in a shift away from traditional instructional models of teaching. Many of the categories in this chapter can be viewed as examples of a constructivist approach, or as being influenced by constructivism.

It has been a very fashionable approach, which always brings its share of problems. Some of the potential drawbacks of a constructivist approach are:

● It can be a smokescreen for poor teaching. By labelling a course approach constructivist, some educators feel they can withdraw and leave the students to do the work. If, after all, there is no wrong answer, then what need is there for the educator? In fact a constructivist approach requires a high degree of input to guide students and frame meaningful activities.
● It can be frustrating for students. Many students, particularly those who are inexperienced learners, find the refusal of constructivist educators to give what they perceive as a straight answer frustrating and detrimental to their learning. They may come through this, but if they feel they are being abandoned to work everything out for themselves they will not find the experience rewarding.
● It can lead to mistaken beliefs. Contrary to what hardcore constructivists may suggest, there are right and wrong beliefs in many topics, as highlighted above. Without the appropriate educator input, the group as a whole might adopt the beliefs of the most dominant member, who might hold views which are factually incorrect.
● It can be time-consuming. A straightforward instructional approach is often the most efficient means of imparting standard knowledge. A constructivist approach can take much longer because it requires students to engage in dialogue or activities that require a longer timescale. They may have to pass through several phases of understanding of concepts before they arrive at the ones that could have been imparted in a text or lecture from the outset. Their understanding and appreciation of this concept may, however, be deeper.

My personal view on constructivism is that it offers a useful background for developing an online pedagogy, but one should sometimes be wary of its promises. It can be used successfully in conjunction with more traditional approaches to achieve the best of both.

Resource based learning

In the story 'The Library of Babel', Luis Borges describes an infinite library composed of hexagonal rooms, and filled with innumerable books whose content is made up of a set of 23 symbols, the meaning of which is often undecipherable:

> The Library is total and that its shelves register all the possible combinations of the twenty-odd orthographical symbols... in other words, all that is given to express, in all languages. Everything.
>
> *(Borges, 1964: 81)*

The Net seems to resemble this library at times in terms of content, and like the librarians in Borges' tale, you may find that locating the information you require seems a hopeless task. Luckily for us, the library that the Net constitutes does not have to be searched physically and we have software to help us. Such a vast pool, if it can be searched effectively, represents a tremendous educational resource, which is why resource based learning has become an increasingly popular pedagogy. As its name suggests, this approach encourages students to use a variety of resources to develop their understanding, rather than a specified few provided by the educator. Students must find out about a topic from a variety of sources, including the Web, discussion, books and journals.

Some of the advantages a resource-based approach offers are that it:

- Encompasses a broad range of students. The variety of resources available means the different learning styles, preferences and needs of individual students can be accommodated, since the students will find resources that best suit those requirements.
- Exposes students to a variety of views. Students can see different viewpoints and appreciate the arguments in any given topic, and not just those given to them.
- Encourages students to be curious and questioning. Related to the above, the students do not just accept the information provided by an educator, but instead develop a curiosity about the knowledge in any topic.
- Develops information skills. Given the oft-quoted phrase about living in an information age, there is a need to develop appropriate skills that allow students to find, analyse and evaluate information from a variety of sources. These are important skills in becoming lifelong learners.
- Promotes active learning. Students have actively to seek out the knowledge, and evaluate it once they find it. They are not passive recipients of knowledge,

but rather engaged in a research-type activity. Playing a more active role in the learning process is generally thought to promote deeper learning.

● Maintains the currency of a course. The up to date resources available online mean that some of the pressure is removed from the educator continually to update the course. If appropriate assignments are set, students can investigate current topics each successive year.

A resource based approach may be realized through the creation of one or more activities, which students perform as individuals or in groups, in which they must solve a problem or produce an output by working with a range of resources. For example, students could be asked to work in groups to produce a Web site that itself acts as a resource for people interested in the influence of Jane Austen on modern literature. The structure of the site might be prescribed, so for example it should contain a page on film adaptations of her works, another on her direct successors, another on her narrative style, and so forth. The resources might be provided to students, such as access to a database of articles, or a collection of resources on CD, or they might simply be left to find their own, with some suggestions as to where and how to look. The educator has an important role here in offering guidance and ensuring that they remain focused on the task and do not get sidetracked.

Since it places the student at the centre of the approach and leaves the educator to perform a facilitative role, this is obviously a constructivist-type methodology. As such it is prone to the same disadvantages listed above. It can again be time-consuming and frustrating for students if they have to examine a lot of resources in detail to find relevant ones. In addition one of the benefits often cited is the development of information skills. If this is the primary benefit, then it may be an approach that is not suitable across a whole curriculum, but rather as a single course. It can provide a useful framework for students to engage with a topic in a meaningful sense, however.

Collaborative learning

As mentioned in the previous chapter, for many educators the ability to be able to implement collaborative learning is reason enough for adopting an online approach. If one takes the view that the Net is a communication medium, rather than a delivery one, then some form of collaborative activity is a logical conclusion. For some, if the Internet is the question, then collaborative learning is the answer. The musician Wynton Marsalis said of jazz, 'the art is in the negotiation'. Much the same might be said of this approach – the learning is in the collaboration, and it will be a different experience with each group of students.

Collaborative learning is another approach that has grown out of constructivist principles. The underlying philosophy is that learning is a social process. The proposed advantages of collaborative learning are that it promotes:

- Reflection. Because students have to explain their ideas or their work, this forces them to look at it reflectively and improve their own knowledge.
- Active learning. As with the other approaches listed here, group work requires students actively to do something with the knowledge, rather than being passive recipients of it.
- Development of communication skills. Working in a group can be a difficult skill to develop, but it is one that students will probably encounter in their working lives, and one for which employees want to see evidence. So it is useful to give students the ability to develop these skills as part of their overall education.
- Deeper understanding. Working collaboratively can improve each student's understanding of the concept, even that of the strongest student, compared with that gained working individually. There is a Gestalt effect, the whole being greater than the sum of the parts.
- Broader scope. Each student can bring something different to the task, whether it is a skill, or knowledge he or she has acquired specifically for the activity. The group can thus cover a broader range of topics, read more articles or achieve tasks that could not have been done individually in the given time.
- Exposure to different ideas. As with resource based learning, collaborative learning can mean students are exposed to different viewpoints, as their fellow students have different concepts and experiences.

Collaborative learning is implemented through group tasks that require students to work as a team or to contribute elements. Gary Alexander (1998) states, 'The job of the educator or instructional designer then is not simply to create materials in which concepts are clearly explained, but to create learning situations in which students find themselves actively engaging with the concepts they are learning.'

For example, students can be given articles or texts to read and discuss as a group, perhaps arriving at some group summary. More ambitiously, students can be given an overall task to achieve, to which they must all contribute, such as creating a group Web site. They can then be guided to a greater or lesser extent in the roles they perform in the task completion. Another popular realization of group work is to use the different members to accomplish more than can be done individually. For instance, they might be given the task of researching a broad topic, with each member researching a different aspect of that topic, bringing back his or her findings and summarizing them for the group.

Hiltz (1997) talks of a 'virtual classroom' where students engage in collaborative activities online. Such activities include

> the 'seminar' type of interchange in which the students become the teachers. Individuals or small groups of students are responsible for making a selection of a topic; reading material not assigned to the rest of the class; preparing a written summary for the class of the most important ideas in the material; and leading a discussion on the topic or material for which they are responsible.

... Another example is to assign students to identify key concepts or skills in each module of the course, make up a question suitable for an exam to test mastery of this material, and answer each other's questions. Exams then actually include selections from the student-generated questions. Students are thus made partners in deciding what it is that is important to know related to course topics, and summarizing this key knowledge. Other examples of collaborative learning strategy... include debates, group projects, case study discussions, simulation and role-playing exercises, 'ask an expert', sharing of solutions to homework problems, and collaborative composition of essays, stories, or research plans.

Suffice to say though that group work is not without its pitfalls. The most common ones include:

- Reluctance and resistance from some students who prefer to work individually.
- Groups that do not gel because of lack of input or personality clashes.
- The time taken to perform group tasks can be excessive if there is a lot of debate and negotiation about which roles people will adopt.
- Excessive time spent deciding upon task allocation, and resentment from members who feel they have done more of the work.
- How to cope with students who drop out of the activity or course.
- When it does not work well, the 'failure' of the group can become the overriding concern for students, and this can be damaging for their learning experience (although there are valuable lessons to be learnt when a group does not work).
- Loss of independence. Many students prefer to work at their own pace and independently of others. This is particularly the case with distance education, where students can set their own pace, often determined by other factors outside education, such as work commitments and holidays. The most serious disadvantage of collaborative work is that some of this independence and flexibility is lost.

All of the above can apply equally to face to face group work. Implementing collaborative learning online raises some additional issues. There is some debate whether the group functions best when it is totally online, or with a mixture of face to face. An early face to face meeting, which allows students to negotiate roles and bond socially, can facilitate the online activity. However, if not all the students can attend a face to face meeting, those who have not done so may feel disadvantaged.

One of the key aspects in the participation of students in collaborative work, and in how they perceive the experience, is how it relates to assessment. In general, for such tasks to be successful they must in some way be linked to assessment. A delicate balance is required here, so students who feel they are in a poor group do not feel they are being punished unjustly. This can be achieved by allocating a portion of the marks to the group element, but the majority to the individual contribution, or requiring reflection upon the group work process as the assessed component. We shall look at this further in the chapter on assessment.

In order to implement collaborative learning successfully, Alexander suggests there are two key components:

- Course design based around collaborative activities in which students engage with the concepts being taught. Learning materials should support these activities rather than be an end in themselves.
- Creating and nurturing a sense of online community and skills of collaboration for the students. This will not happen automatically by itself.

Although difficult, possibly time-consuming and occasionally frustrating, collaborative learning offers a number of benefits that make it an almost essential part of any online course that sets out to use the technology in a meaningful way. However, my personal feeling is that it should be implemented with caution. The requirement for students to work collaboratively does run counter to the flexibility offered by distance study, since students are tied to the specific timing of activities. If students find themselves involved in a different group task every week, it can be tiring and frustrating. Thus providing a combination of collaborative activities, appropriately spaced throughout the course, and individual activities can provide the benefits of both approaches.

Problem based learning

This approach works by turning the conventional teaching process on its head. It starts with the problem, rather than providing the information and then providing a problem to test understanding. Students are given an 'ill-structured problem', that is, a problem for which they do not currently possess enough information to reach a solution. This then requires them to find the appropriate information and to gain any skills necessary to solve the problem.

Some of the possible advantages of problem based learning (PBL) are:

- Increased student motivation. Gaining knowledge in order to solve a specific problem provides a tangible purpose to the learning process.
- Development of problem solving skills. Such a course obviously provides an opportunity for students to develop general problem solving skills, although this does require assistance and guidance from the educator.
- Increased student responsibility. Students have to take responsibility for finding the appropriate information and developing a realistic solution to the problem.
- Flexibility. Students can develop different solutions to the problem, given their particular interests and knowledge.

- Exposure to different ideas and solutions. By sharing information and eventual solutions, students can gain a broad appreciation of the subject area.
- Contextualization of information. When information is used within a meaningful context, abstract ideas and concepts have an increased significance.
- Interactive and engaging. Students need to be very active in this mode of learning, since they need to drive the experience themselves. This activity, reflection and analysis can lead to a deeper understanding of the problem than is acquired through more passive methods of learning.

PBL can take place individually or in groups. It can take the form of traditional research projects (indeed all research can be seen as PBL), or smaller problems which force students to think through the issues involved. The key is that the learning is problem driven.

Online this can be a successful approach because students can discuss issues, find the information required, present their solutions and so on. It can also be realized through interactive simulations or virtual worlds, where students are presented with a problem. For example, in electrical engineering students can build virtual circuits or equipment that will solve a specified problem. When failure occurs they can be presented with information or hints why that solution failed, thus leading them to an eventual solution.

Some of the potential drawbacks of problem based learning include:

- Uncertainty on the part of students. It may not be clear to students exactly what they need to do in order to gain certain grades since there is no 'right answer'. They may also be unsure how they should proceed, since this approach requires them to take more responsibility for their learning than may have been the case previously.
- Time-consuming. Students can spend an excessive amount of time in 'blind alleys' or in locating the information they need. This is, of course, true of all research, so educator guidance can avoid this. If students are new to PBL they will need a lot of support, so it can be time-consuming for the educator also.
- Loss of focus. Students can spend excessive time trying to second guess what answer the educator 'wants'. In this case they need to be encouraged to take ownership of the problem and to appreciate that there may not be a single right answer. They may also become focused on a side issue, or on the nature of PBL itself.
- Suitability. It might not be suitable for all topics: for instance, it is not suitable when there definitely are right answers, or any problems are too complex for students to solve without more initial formal teaching.

PBL does require quite a substantial rethink in terms of course approach. It is a practical approach, since it places the assessment as the driving factor. This is in reality how many students operate. The assessment at the end of a course represents the problem to be solved, and they engage in trying to gain the information required to solve it, for instance by learning and revising only those subjects that they think will arise in the exam. If the problem is placed at the start of the course and used to drive the learning, students can spend less time trying to guess what information they will need and instead can engage with the topic. The result can be more rewarding for both students and educators alike.

Narrative based teaching

Narrative can be used in a variety of ways in education. It is a powerful method, based on a well developed human capacity to absorb, remember and understand stories. There are differing interpretations of the term 'narrative', but for the purpose of this section let us take it to mean a story, plus the discourse, that is the mode of telling the story. Stories are well used in primary and secondary education, but less explicitly in tertiary education. However, if one expands the concept of narrative to encompass more than an explicit story, then educational explanations, which make use of models, histories or case studies, can all be said to be using a narrative approach. Narrative can be used for different purposes in education:

- To make a subject more memorable. By placing the content within a narrative the educator utilizes a well-developed capacity for storage and comprehension in most people.
- To provide structure. A narrative can be used to bring together concepts and facts into a cohesive whole.
- To provide a familiar format. If the subject is unfamiliar and the medium also (for example, the Net for many people) then the use of narrative provides a familiar and comfortable format.
- To provide context. It can be difficult for students to grasp abstract concepts without some context to see how they are realized in the 'real world'. Narrative or anecdotes can be useful in providing this meaningful context.
- To make a subject more interesting. Related to some of the above, many students struggle with difficult or abstract concepts, or 'dry' subjects. Narrative can be a way of making the subject 'come alive' for students.

Narrative is the sort of device many educators use without much need for thought, for example by telling anecdotes during a lecture. I still remember being told that the anthropologist Benjamin Lee Whorf was a fire prevention officer. Such incidental details made a difficult concept (the Sapir–Whorf hypothesis, that language determines what a person perceives and thinks about the world) more memorable (to the extent that I could answer an exam question on it, anyway).

When teaching shifts to an online environment, like so much else about the transition from face to face education, it requires an explicit intention to include narrative. This can be done in several ways, for instance by using a compelling narrative to drive the course. This is what we have done with T171. To teach about the technology of computers and the Internet as well as their impact upon society, we chose two textbooks which had a strong narrative, that dealt with the history of the development of these technologies. This provided a central thread from which we could explore a range of topics. It also helped provide context and interest to a subject area many students find rather dry. Other ways of including narrative in the content are to provide real accounts to enliven each subject. A popular method in certain subject areas is to use a case based approach, which provides students with a series of real or imaginary cases, which they must use to interpret abstract principles or draw conclusions. As with resource based learning, the wealth of such information available makes this an attractive approach for online courses. This is particularly appealing in certain subject areas that use cases to extract rules and principles such as law, medicine and business.

Narrative can also be used as a means of structuring activities. By providing students with a scenario, or a narrative in which they act, you can make the task meaningful. For instance, you could create a scenario in which groups of students have to develop e-commerce proposals which will undergo a stock market evaluation. Alternatively, students can be asked to construct a narrative within which they have to incorporate certain elements. There is research (eg Plowman, 1996) that indicates that in a non-linear environment such as multi-media or the Web, navigation itself can become the focus. In this situation students focus on navigating, on surface tasks such as clicking buttons and experimenting with tools. A task that is structured around a narrative creates a linear path in a non-linear environment, which is relevant for online courses.

The disadvantages of a narrative approach are as follows:

- The narrative itself can become the focus. If a powerful narrative is used there is a danger that the details of the narrative will obscure the academic content. To use my example, this would mean that I remember Whorf was a fire officer, but nothing of the Sapir–Whorf hypothesis.
- It might offer only one view. Some narrative approaches will not provide the range of views that is a benefit of some of the other approaches in this chapter. Because the narrative itself must occupy a significant part of the course content, this provides less opportunity for exploring different viewpoints. A case based approach, however, can offer a range of arguments and experiences. In general, though, a narrative based approach is more didactic than constructivist.
- It can be less interactive. A course based largely around reading a narrative is a less interactive approach than the ones outlined above, although interactivity can be built in: for example, through group work or discussion.

Like many approaches, narrative can be adopted to a greater or lesser extent. It can be merely a way of enlivening one particular topic, a means of structuring an activity or the main theme for the course. It has always been a powerful educational tool, and will no doubt continue to be so in an online environment, although the form it takes here will be subtly transformed.

Situated learning

The situated learning approach comes from the work of Lave and Wenger, in particular their book of the same name (Lave and Wenger, 1991). It also draws upon the work of Brown and others (eg Brown, Collins and Duguid, 1989) in describing cognitive apprenticeships, so I will group the two together for convenience.

The theory behind situated learning is that people learn best through what Lave and Wenger call 'legitimate peripheral participation': that is, partaking in activities within a community that are valid, but not central. Many formal and informal apprenticeships fall into this category. Lave and Wenger provide several examples, including Yucatec midwives. In this society midwives usually come from the same family. The midwife starts as a young girl listening to stories and is immersed in the everyday life of a midwife. Later she will accompany her mother or grandmother on visits, and eventually help out in some small tasks. She will take on more tasks, and eventually the full birth. This is completely informal, and without any direct teaching. In Lave and Wenger's term she moves from peripheral to central participation. The notion of a 'community of practice' is important also: that is, people learn within a community of other learners and experts. Lave and Wenger claim that 'It seems typical of apprenticeship that apprentices learn mostly in relation with other apprentices.' It is, then, important that the learner has some valid form of participation in this community. Learning is thus situated within a culture and context and cannot be separated out from this as formal education tries to do. The learning is also incidental, rather than deliberate.

This is an interesting theory, and one that has radical implications for the way in which education is conducted. It emphasizes the informal nature of learning, and also the extended timeframe over which education occurs. It is, however, rather difficult to implement within existing educational frameworks. How do you make learning incidental, and if you do create such an environment, how can you be sure that learning will take place? Young (1993) outlines four tasks in implementing situated learning:

- The creation of situations that involve the learner in realistic problem solving.
- The provision of 'scaffolding': that is, guidance and help which will enable new learners to become more adept.
- Repositioning of the educator's role as facilitator.
- Assessing the growth of the individuals and the community as a whole.

In practice this approach has led to a more community based course, where students are encouraged to interact with each other. The role of the educator becomes more open: for instance, students might watch as the educator works through an actual problem, instead of being given a completed answer. The activities are intended to be legitimate, peripheral ones, that have some meaning: for example, a research based approach or solving real problems that face those working in a particular field. It is the notion of a community of practice that has attracted most interest for online courses. The use of online communication allows students to participate in discussions with actual practitioners: for example, software engineering students might subscribe and participate in newsgroups focused on a particular programming language, to which those working in the area contribute.

Situated learning is important for the emphasis it places on co-participation within a community, rather than learning as something that takes place within individuals. It is somewhat difficult to classify as an approach in itself, since, as Lave and Wenger stress, 'legitimate peripheral participation is not in itself an educational form, much less a pedagogical strategy or teaching technique. It is an analytical viewpoint on learning, a way of understanding learning' (Lave and Wenger, 1991: 40). I have included it here because the notion of a community of practice within which learners can participate has particular relevance on the Net, which is a medium built around communities.

Lessons for implementation

I have been rather selective in the approaches I have outlined above, and also rather scant in my coverage of them. I have not included some approaches that many might have expected to be here. Partly this is because some of this can be seen as subsumed in the approaches I have mentioned, and partly because of the need to be selective. I have chosen approaches that I feel work well on the Net, but this is by no means an exclusive list. The intention is to provide an overview of the type of approaches which are implemented successfully on the Net, and the reasons why they are relevant online. In doing so, I have ignored whole areas of debate and simplified complex issues, but I hope you have gained a flavour of the approaches. There is a great deal of overlap between approaches, and indeed many people will not agree with the categorizations I have used. What most of these approaches have in common is that they are student centred and require a lot of interaction. I have neglected to include the standard instructional approach, that is, teaching primarily through text or lectures. This is because this is the norm, and most courses will include an element of this. It is also an approach that, if adopted in isolation, fails to take advantage of what the Net offers, namely the opportunity for interaction and communication.

Some of the broader lessons for implementation are outlined below.

I   Select an appropriate pedagogy

In order to successfully deliver an online course you need a strong pedagogical strategy. This may require much more thought and reflection than is perhaps usually given to a traditional lecture series (in terms of the approach itself, rather than the actual content).

The pedagogical approach implemented in any one course will be influenced by a number of factors including:

● the personal tastes and beliefs of the educator;
● what approach is best suited to the type of material and skills required in that topic;
● the level at which the course is being taught;
● experiences students may have had on other courses;
● the types of students on a particular course and their needs and beliefs;
● the resources (in terms of people, time, money and learning materials) and technology available.

2   Combine approaches

Many approaches can be combined successfully within one course. This not only means that each can be used where it is best suited, but also makes for an interesting course. The danger is that students feel they have just become comfortable with one approach when a new one is thrust upon them, which can be disruptive. However, many of the approaches are complementary. For instance, a collaborative activity can be implemented within any course, or narrative used as part of a situated approach.

3   Be prepared to take a different role

What most of the approaches above have in common is that they place the educator in a much more supportive, less central role. The educator's function is now first to create the learning opportunities and then to guide students through these, while allowing the students to be active in the learning process. This is quite a fundamental shift for many educators, and it has been suggested that it is one that rather undermines the ego of some. It is significant on the Net, however, since the medium is not suited to being dominated by one individual, but rather is a technology which facilitates communication from all participants. The popularity of constructivist type approaches in online courses is partly a result of this.

4   Utilize the strengths of the technology

This is repeating what I have stressed in previous chapters, but the Net has several characteristics that are beneficial in education. First, it gives access to a wide range of resources. Second, it allows communication between students, educators and professionals to occur in a manner that makes interaction more likely (for instance by not having to arrange physical meetings) and encourages reflective contributions. Lastly, it gives flexibility as to time and distance. Unless the course content is itself focused on some aspects of the Net, then the course pedagogy should be taking advantage of at least two of these factors, otherwise the question will be asked why that course is being delivered online.

Conclusion

The Net offers certain features that make the approaches covered here both more suitable and desirable from a learning perspective. The interactive nature of the Net means that, unlike with many previous educational technologies, the educator can adapt the material and offer support while the course is in progress, rather than just relying on the material embedded within the technology itself (as for example with a CD ROM).

If such approaches represent a departure for many educators, this also applies for many students, who have often been schooled in the traditional 'chalk and talk' approach. This can result in both frustration and resentment on the part of the student. Much of the focus can be centred on the approach itself rather than the topic in question. In this respect educators have a duty to both structure courses so as to minimize such feelings, for instance by giving clear indications as to what is expected from students, and offer ongoing support and guidance, for instance during group work. It may also be necessary to consider the level of the students, so that more radical approaches are reserved for more experienced learners. Similarly, the degree to which any approach is implemented can vary. There are courses with very strong constructivist or resource based approaches, which do not provide any material to the students, whereas others may offer a specific database or set of materials, along with more guidance.

When dealing with any educational technology there is a strong link between the pedagogy and the possibilities of the technology itself. In a later chapter we will look at some of the different technologies available and discuss how they can be implemented in courses.

In the next chapter the theme of communication stressed by many of the pedagogies outlined here is continued.

Summary

In this chapter, six approaches to online teaching have been outlined in terms of their underlying theory and implementation. Some of the advantages and disadvantages of each approach have been highlighted. The six pedagogical approaches were:

- constructivism;
- resource based learning;
- collaborative learning;
- problem based learning;
- narrative based learning;
- situated learning.

From this coverage four lessons for implementation were drawn:

- Select an appropriate pedagogy.
- Combine approaches.
- Be prepared to take a different role.
- Utilize the strengths of the technology.

Chapter 6

Communication

Introduction

Much of the research focus in online education has been on computer mediated communication (CMC). How does this differ from face to face communication? How should one conduct online activities? How does it affect student performance and behaviour?

In this chapter we will look at some of these issues and some effective uses of the medium. If one views the Net as a two-way medium, then CMC is the vital ingredient in any online course. It is the glue which holds together the rest of the course components. Therefore gaining an appreciation of the different forms it takes and ways of implementing it successfully within a course is necessary for the successful delivery of any online course.

The manner in which CMC is implemented will have a strong influence on the way students interact with each other and how they engage with the course as a whole. CMC is taken here to include all forms of communication technology mediated through the Net that promote dialogue, for example e-mail, asynchronous text-based conferences, synchronous text chat, and video conferencing. This does not include straightforward Web pages since they are less about dialogue and more about the transmission of content.

Differences from face to face communication

In order to appreciate what constitutes good online communication it is necessary to appreciate how it differs from face to face interaction. This will depend on the type of CMC being used. Let us suppose it is text-based e-mail or conferencing, which constitutes the majority of CMC implementation. This medium differs from face to face communication in a number of ways:

- It lacks many of the subtle communication cues present in face to face situations. Facial expressions, vocal tones and body language are all used in face to face communication to supplement the actual content of the verbal communication.
- It is asynchronous. Much e-mail and conferencing takes place asynchronously, although real-time chat is also used. The asynchronous nature of the communication has a great number of benefits in education, which will be explored later.
- It has a relative anonymity. Even when the sender of a message is known socially to the readers, the online environment adds an element of anonymity to the communication. This can be liberating for many people who find it difficult to communicate in face to face situations when they become the centre of attention.
- It has a greater reach. A message in a conference can be read by a far wider audience than might hear a comment from a student in a face to face setting.

What are the implications of these differences? First, the loss of much of the additional information present in face to face interaction has resulted in the development of effective online communication skills, or Netiquette. The most obvious of these are the smileys used by online communicators to indicate when they are joking, being sarcastic or whatever. These are a useful, but rather blatant attempt to convey some of the information usually transmitted through non-verbal cues. What is probably more significant is the development and improvement of appropriate writing skills. The tone of a written message can convey as much as face to face cues if it is well written and if the reader is adept at picking up on these cues. This is a skill only developed through experience, combined with reflection. The general improvement of writing (and reading) skills is of benefit in the educational arena, and the medium can provide a meaningful and social context in which students can do this.

The asynchronous nature of CMC is significant in education because it fosters a flexible learning approach, which is less fixed to a specific time pattern than traditional campus based models. This is important because as we saw in earlier chapters, part of the power of the Net is its ability to appeal to different types of students, with different needs. The phrase 'asynchronous learning network' (ALN) is widely used to refer to educational environments which operate in an asynchronous manner and have a strong emphasis on interaction. The ALN Web site defines them as:

Asynchronous learning networks (ALN) are people networks for anytime – anywhere learning. ALN combines self-study with substantial, rapid, asynchronous interactivity with others. In ALN learners use computer and communications technologies to work with remote learning resources, including coaches and other learners, but without the requirement to be online at the same time.

(http://www.aln.org/alnweb/aln.htm)

The asynchronous factor also allows students to think about their answers and respond in a more considered fashion than many find possible in a real-time situation. Vladimir Nabokov once commented, 'I think like a genius, I write like a distinguished author, and I speak like a child'. While few of us think or write like Nabokov, most people suffer the same relative scale of quality of expression. The written mode facilitates a more reflective and informed debate, which benefits not only those partaking in it, but those who read it also.

The anonymity of the medium is an interesting phenomenon. I do not mean total anonymity with false user names (this happens on the Net a lot and can have intriguing consequences, but is rare in educational contexts). Rather it is the relative anonymity the medium affords the sender compared with speaking in the presence of peers. Many users find this liberating, since they would feel intimidated in front of an actual audience, but feel they can contribute successfully in an online environment. Also, many people who may be disadvantaged in the face to face situation are empowered in the virtual world. People with a speech impediment can be heard clearly, there is no advantage given to the good-looking people in the class, those with uninteresting voices can be witty and entertaining, and so on. The medium changes the dynamics of the social interactions, which is to the benefit of many people. It will equally disempower others, for instance those who do not like writing, or who suffer from dyslexia, or who were previously empowered in a face to face situation. The anonymity factor can have its downside also. It is much easier to complain, to be aggressive or dominate a conference when you do not have to meet others physically. However, the technology also provides us with means of dealing with this, since such users can be banned from a conference, given 'read only' status, or more likely, the other users can simply choose not to read their messages.

This relates to the last point regarding the extension of reach. In an online conference students can 'hear' from a far wider range of students than they might do in the face to face context. It is easy to send a message which is going to be read by one person, 10 people or 100 people. The act is much the same, whereas speaking to these different numbers of people creates vastly different social pressures and requires different techniques. The range of students who might make vocal contributions in a face to face course can be limited to those who are socially confident, whereas potentially more students can contribute on an online course. This again can have its problems, since some students now have a larger audience for their grievances. The proportion of active participants, particularly in large conferences, is unlikely to include all students. There are three, or potentially four, types of online behaviour in conferences:

- Active participants. These people send and respond to a lot of messages, on a very regular basis. They will be the most common names in the conference.
- Partially active participants. These students will read most, but probably not all messages, and occasionally respond or send an initial query or message.
- Lurkers. A term many people do not like in education since they feel it has a value suggestion, but it is one common on the Net. These people rarely, if ever, contribute, but regularly read messages.

The last category one might wish to include is those who do not read or contribute at all: but depending on the course structure, such behaviour is sometimes impossible if the student is to pass the course. There is nearly always a mix of these behaviours, and in their way each plays a significant role in the conference and in turn gains something from it. Many people try to discourage lurking. If this occurs during a collaborative task, then this is understandable, since all the students should contribute. If, however, it is in a more general discussion conference, or part of the ongoing course, then lurking is a justified and valid behaviour, since it provides an audience for the participants and it provides the lurker with a broad range of views.

Synchronous communication

The previous section focused on asynchronous communication. This usually takes the form of e-mail between individuals, mailing lists, public spaces such as conferences, newsgroups, bulletin boards and so on, and shared areas where users can work jointly on documents and files.

Asynchronous communication is implemented on the majority of online courses, mainly because of the benefits highlighted above. To these should be added reliability: because it is predominantly text-based, such communication is very robust over the Net using low bandwidth and standard modems. Synchronous communication technologies are used in some courses, and these have a number of different issues associated with them. Synchronous CMC might incorporate any of the following:

- real-time text chat, either between individuals or in a 'chat room';
- audio conferencing between two or more individuals;
- video conferencing between two or more individuals;
- shared workspaces such as whiteboards.

Over the past few years the technology of instant messaging has become increasingly popular. This is real-time text-based communication using software provided by companies such as AOL, Microsoft and Yahoo. Instant messaging allows the user to create a list of contacts who also use the same software. Whenever those people come online the user is notified and can engage in a real-time conversation. Initially popular with younger users, it has become widely used within organizations. This is partly because it operates outside the formal communication channels, so is less prone to monitoring than e-mail. It is also related to the type of conversations such a system engenders. The always-on access provided at work makes real-time communication ideal for chat, gossip, quick exchanges and so on – in short, the informal sort of exchanges that often occur in corridors and around coffee machines. This social element of instant messaging could have useful implications in online education, enabling remote students to engage in some of the informal communication which is an important component of campus education. It could also be useful in structured activities such as collaborative group work.

As mentioned above, asynchronous communication has a number of benefits, particularly with regard to flexibility in learning. However, synchronous communication also has a number of benefits. These can be summarized as:

- Time saving. Using synchronous communication particularly for tasks that require negotiation, such as deciding upon group roles, can reduce the time taken to complete a task. With asynchronous communication some tasks can take weeks, because students are waiting for a response from one or two individuals, or the time lag between posing questions and receiving responses becomes excessive. One synchronous session can often be useful to perform the initial negotiation or discussion, and then asynchronous communication can be used for the remainder of the task.
- Social identity. Particularly with video and audio conferencing, many of the communication cues absent in asynchronous communication are again present. This can be useful for creating a social identity for the group members, which may be different from that in asynchronous communication. This is not always beneficial, as indicated below.
- Suitability for some subject areas. There are some topics where synchronous communication is essential in gaining the necessary skills. Learning a foreign language is an obvious example, and here audio or video conferencing can be very useful in developing speaking and listening ability. Similarly some management topics might require interaction in real time.
- Creating an event. In order to create an event there needs to be a feeling that the student is participating in something that is occurring now, and not simply revisiting a past event. For example, a presentation from a guest speaker can be followed up by a real-time question and answer session. These can be archived for later reference, but the synchronous nature of the communication creates the sense of being actively involved in the event.

Synchronous communication therefore offers a number of potential benefits. However, since it removes one of the key advantages Net based education offers, that is flexibility in study patterns, it should probably be used with caution. In addition it has some other disadvantages that should be borne in mind when implementing it:

● Bandwidth and quality. Real-time text chat works well over the Net, although using it effectively is something of an acquired skill. Audio conferencing has a loss in quality if more than a few people are using it over standard modems. Video conferencing is generally poor quality unless one is using a dedicated high-bandwidth network: for instance, video conferencing suites. This makes it useful for specific link-ups with distant institutions but means students have to attend a physical place in order to do so, which removes much of the benefit offered by online education. Individual video conferencing via cheap Web-cams and modem links is poor quality, but can be useful. This will of course become less of an issue as high-bandwidth connections become more commonplace in people's homes or study centres.

● Immediacy of communication. Making the communication synchronous means the possibility to reflect and compose thoughtful messages is lost, along with the benefit this brings for many students.

● Potentially disempowering. Audio and video conferencing have the potential to disempower many people who were empowered by text-based communication as indicated above. Larry Lessig (1999) cites three such groups for whom e-mail and the like has been enabling: the visually impaired, the deaf and the 'ugly' (in a society obsessed by physical looks, he argues, good-looking people have a social advantage in many real situations). Visually impaired people can implement speech programs, deaf people can communicate equally well without the need to hear anything, and the 'ugly' can be gauged on their personality, not their appearance. In more subtle ways the removal of physical presence affects the communication of all users, often beneficially. It at least creates a space that is different from all other spaces. When video conferencing is implemented, all of the same characteristics are reintroduced. It makes cyberspace much more like conventional space, which may not necessarily be a good thing. Contrary to what many people think, more is not always better in terms of technology.

Although synchronous communication has a number of advantages, in order to maintain the flexibility of approach and decrease some of the disadvantages it brings, it is usually advisable to implement it in conjunction with asynchronous communication, with the latter forming the main thread of the course. This is, of course, one of the great benefits of the Net, that different forms of communication and media can be combined within the same workspace and in the same course.

Types of computer conference

CMC can be implemented in a number of ways in a course, depending on the pedagogy embodied in the course, the technology used, the topic area, the number of students and so forth. An important point to note is that it does have to be integrated within the course. Merely providing students with e-mail or a bulletin board will not suffice to make it part of the educational experience. Hiltz (1997), who has been influential in the development of the asynchronous learning networks, puts it like this:

> It does not 'work' to simply make an ALN available and tell students that they can use it to ask questions about the readings or discuss aspects of the course at any time. If it is not a 'required' and graded, integral part of the course, the majority of the students will never use it at all; and those who start to use it, will generally decide that 'nothing is going on there' and will stop using it.

This suggests that use of CMC must be integrated into the assessment of the course. This does not necessarily mean that students are graded on contributions to a conference (although this can be done), but could arise from making a group task which requires contributions from all form the main part of assessment. We will look at assessment in a later chapter. Even if the use of CMC is not directly linked to assessment, it does need to be integrated in the course material and approach, rather than merely an add-on, if students and educators are to gain the full benefit it offers.

CMC can be implemented to perform a variety of functions on a course:

- Collaborative work. This is probably the most important function for any course that incorporates a collaborative element.
- Course information. CMC is an obvious means of delivering information, downloadable files, updates and stop presses to students.
- Troubleshooting. Conferences can be provided where students can seek help on specific issues, such as software problems. These are usually moderated by an expert who can answer the queries.
- Social chat. The importance of the social element in any form of study should not be underestimated. Students can interact with other students on the same course, or across the university.
- Course discussion. This can either be a general discussion space to talk about issues that the course raises, or an area where students are given a specific topic to debate and to summarize.
- Broader participation. Students can be made to feel part of a 'virtual campus' by having access to a variety of different conferences in which other students, alumni, staff and invited external people participate. These can mirror the sort of societies and clubs one might find at a conventional university, such as film, football, poetry and computer games.
- Tutor support. On larger courses there may be a number of tutors, and CMC is a useful means of providing support, clarification, answers to course related queries, general feedback and so on.

We have already seen examples of the type of collaborative activities that can be conducted online in the previous chapter. The social function of communication forms an important role in study. Far from being frivolous or detrimental to 'serious' study, it can create a bond between students, which facilitates the group-working process. It also keeps conferences active and acts like a glue, holding elements of the course together for students in a social context. Some courses separate out the social chat into a distinct conference, while others incorporate it within the course conferences (by not providing an explicit separate area for it). There is some evidence that these informal elements are necessary in creating a successful online course, and removing such exchanges to a separate conference may be harmful to the group activities (eg Lebie, Rhoades and McGrath, 1995; Gunawardena and Zittle, 1998), although this will depend on the size of the conference and the task in question. However, different social dynamics can be created by using conferences which have a different membership, for example all the students on a particular course rather than just one tutor group, or an area which is student only, so no faculty members have access.

Similarly, discussion of course related issues can be conducted in a separate conference, or as part of the main conference. This will depend on the number of students on any course. If there is a large cohort, then general discussion is often better served by having all the students in one area. This is partly a function of numbers and contributors. Only a proportion of students will take part in undirected discussion, following the types of contributors outlined above, often in roughly equal proportions. Therefore a larger number of students is needed to achieve a 'critical mass' for active discussion.

If the discussion is more directed and integrated within the course, for example as part of an assessed activity, then smaller groups can partake in more intensive and focused exchanges. Depending on the size of the student cohort, a mixture of these approaches is also possible. The same applies with troubleshooting or help conferences. These might be subsumed as part of the general conference, or they might be separated out. If the conference is dealing with an area that requires particular expertise, for instance software problems, that may be beyond the scope of the educator in charge of the actual course. In such cases a conference with one or more experts available to answer questions, that can be accessed by a number of different courses, can free the educator to focus on course issues. Another benefit of pooling students in this way is that they represent a good knowledge source in themselves, and with sufficiently large numbers other students will offer peer support and advice.

Allowing students to participate in conferences and discussions beyond the specific course is a good means of creating a sense of online community. This adds a sense of richness to online study, which is important for many students. It increases the social benefit students achieve during study and makes the online environment more akin to campus education, in that it is not solely about study, but about personal development and social interaction also.

By way of example, I will outline the conferencing structure on T171 in its

2002 realization, which is similar to that on many OU courses. The first point to stress here is that this is a large scale course, with around 10,000 students annually. Each student has access to the following conferences:

- Student group conference. This is 'controlled' by the student's tutor (Associate Faculty) who is employed on a part-time basis by the OU. Only the tutor and the other 20 or so students in that tutor group have access to this conference. This is where most of the guided activities and discussions take place.
- Noticeboard. Students have read-only access to this. It is used by the course team to make announcements, offer general advice, issue stop-presses, etc.
- Resources and FAQs. These are read-only areas containing FAQs on aspects relating to software, university procedures, the assignment submission process, etc. There are also some university-wide resources, such as the code of conduct, virus software updates, and so on.
- Synchronous chat. This is a chat room, which students can enter at any time, and communicate via real-time text.
- Support conferences. Since part of the course deals with teaching students to use software, there are technical help conferences where students can go and ask questions. These are moderated by experts. We have four conferences dealing with specific types of software.
- Discussion forum. The course material raises questions, which it suggests students might like to discuss in this conference. This does not form part of the assessment, but is used to give students an area where they can discuss issues that interest or puzzle them. It is also moderated so advice can be given.
- Café. This conference is moderated by ex-students (the other moderators are taken from the pool of tutors). It is a general social area where they can talk about course or other matters with a broader range of students than is available in their tutor group conference.

Given the number of students on the course, they have been divided into six subsets, and the conferences replicated, so each subset has its own support conferences, discussion forum and café, which students in the other subset cannot access. This creates a large enough population (around 2,000 students at the course start) in each conference for it to be viable, without the number of messages becoming too difficult to manage. The conference structure for one student subset is shown in Figure 6.1.

However, when this course was adapted for delivery in the United States the number of students was significantly smaller. The larger support and discussion conferences did not have sufficient student numbers to be viable, so the functions of these were implemented within the tutor groups. A café conference, which covered several courses, was adopted instead of a course-specific one.

The conference structure has been altered as the course itself has altered and in light of feedback from students. This makes for a very dynamic course, one that varies each year. In addition the students create much of the course environment

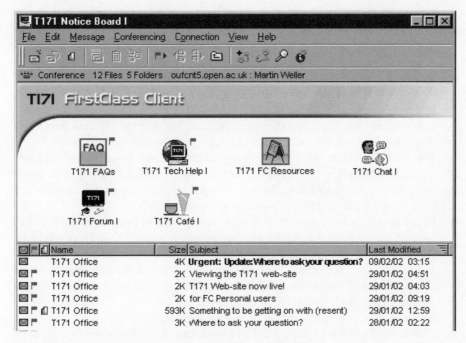

Figure 6.1 *The student conferences on OU course T171*

themselves, so each cohort is different and creates an environment with different characteristics. This is particularly noticeable across the subsets of conferences. Each café, for instance, will develop a 'personality' of its own, which is a function of the most dominant members of the conference and the way the moderators interact with the students also.

Teaching via CMC

What is it like to teach principally via CMC? As I have been stressing throughout this book, it is different in nature from face to face teaching. A number of models of teaching effectively via CMC have been developed. Most concur that the important shift is to a more facilitative role, for the reasons mentioned in the previous chapter. Running a conference, or moderating, requires some delicate skills to deal with issues such as:

● Non-contributors. Some students might not be reading messages or engaging with the group, to their own detriment and that of the group as a whole. They might have valid reasons for doing so (illness, work commitments) or it might be that they simply prefer working individually. If participation is not essential, then non-contributors are less of an issue. If there is a group activity and there are non-contributors, then this might result in the group being unable to fulfil its task, or resentment from other group members. This is part of the learning process in creating successfully working groups, but it requires adept moderating to prevent arguments and resentment from arising.

● Dominant members. Some members of a conference might send so many messages that they end up dominating the group. This can be inhibiting for other contributors. The problem is confounded if these messages are aggressive or dismissive. It is often the case that more knowledgeable members think they are being helpful, but in fact they can make other students feel inferior. This can be dealt with by inviting contributions from other students, speaking privately with the dominant members and asking them to allow some others to contribute first (while praising their own contributions) or even limiting the number of postings per individual.

● Keeping groups on target. It is possible for groups to become sidetracked or focused on small details to the detriment of the overall task. Depending on the amount of guidance the course embodies, students can either be left to realize this for themselves (and thus perhaps learn a valuable lesson about group working) or gently guided so that the group progresses. The latter approach, although usually preferable, needs to be done in a manner which does not detract from the value of anyone's input.

● Maintaining a friendly, supportive environment. As well as dealing with anti-social behaviour such as bullying or aggressiveness, the moderator needs to encourage all students to contribute and to help each other. This might mean not answering each question that is raised but rather allowing, or encouraging, other students to offer their opinions or advice. This will often lead to a fruitful debate, whereas a single query that is answered by the educator often goes no further, since this is seen as the 'right answer'. By encouraging regular input from students and responding in a friendly manner, the moderator sets the tone of the conference and encourages students to contribute at any time, without feeling their posting is not important enough, or is irrelevant.

● Creating tasks which engage students. Perhaps more so than campus based students, those online have competing demands on their time, particularly if they are studying part-time. Therefore, the educator needs to create tasks which are interesting and enjoyable, and have a motivation which can compete with other demands. As well as creating such tasks, the educator needs to support and encourage students during their performance.

The reaction of educators accustomed to face to face teaching might be that they are currently responsible for a lot more. While they would be responsible for maintaining an appropriate environment in a one-hour lecture, say, their responsibility would not normally extend beyond this. The asynchronous nature of the communication results in the removal of discrete time slots such as the lecture, and the educator is responsible for something with a life that spans the whole duration of the course.

   This raises another difference with face to face teaching, namely time commitment. It might not necessarily be more (or less) in an online environment, but it will be more distributed. Instead of one or more one-hour lectures per week, with some follow-up, educators might find themselves checking an online course for 15 minutes every day. Conflicts, crises and questions can arise very quickly in an online environment, so leaving it for a week, say, might find the educator returning to a conference filled with messages on a particular topic. I have painful memories of the time when a false rumour about T171 claimed it would be worth more in terms of study credit points the following year. This started in one conference and some students suggested they demand that it be upgraded now. The first posting was about 5 pm and by 9 pm it had spread to all of the subsets of conferences, some university-wide ones, several tutor groups and a number of the course team, with each new student posting his or her outrage and support for the campaign. We spent a good deal of time 'chasing' the rumour and explaining it was entirely untrue. Like forest fires, whenever we thought it had been beaten it would flare up quickly and unexpectedly elsewhere. Had some of the moderators not acted quickly it would have reached epidemic proportions, and been quite damaging to the student experience if it had gone unnoticed for several days.
   There are a number of models of conducting online activities and effective moderating. One that is commonly cited and adopted is Gilly Salmon's (2000) five-stage model. This proposes that developing the appropriate skills to learn online requires time and exposure. If activities are implemented that address each level within the framework of a course (or courses), students can be guided through the successive stages. At each stage different e-moderating skills are required. The stages are as follows:

1. Access and motivation. This stage focuses on gaining access to and using the CMC system. These are the pragmatic issues of setting up software, getting connected and sending some messages. At this stage the moderator needs to provide technical help, and also welcome students online and create a motivation for participation. It ends when participants have posted their first messages.
2. Online socialization. This is induction and socialization within the online environment. At this stage the students become accustomed to sending messages and the rules of behaviour in this environment. Moderators need to provide bridges between known forms of behaviour and this often new environment. They need to encourage all participants to feel comfortable sending messages and expressing views. This stage is over, according to Salmon, when participants begin to 'share a little of themselves online'.
3. Information exchange. At this stage students ask for and give information. This is a useful stage for many students, and often this is the level at which they remain. At this stage students request information of the tutor or other students, for example regarding an assignment, and freely exchange

information. Overload may occur at this stage, and the moderator's task is to help students develop strategies for dealing with the amount of information available. He or she should encourage participants to use the learning resources and exchange information regarding them.

4. Knowledge construction. At this stage the group works together with a specific outcome, and with different roles, interacting in more participative ways. The moderator here may start the tasks, and contribute to discussion, but he or she has a supportive, non-authoritative role.

5. Development. At this stage students are responsible for their own learning, and need little support.

This model can be implemented in an online course to ensure students progress to a meaningful level of communication. It does raise the issue of modularity in courses. For example, is it necessary for all courses to implement stage 1, when many students will be familiar with the software from previous courses? If one cannot guarantee this familiarity, then it is, but this may be frustrating for students who have extensive online experience. Welcoming students and encouraging early socialization is always important, but these early stages may take less time with more experienced students. Certainly as online study becomes more commonplace, it will be less important to treat students as if this were a new context for many courses.

Lessons for implementation

Teaching via CMC involves creating a different environment from the one to which educators and students are accustomed. This has its own set of demands and behaviours, but also its own distinct benefits. Implementing and moderating a successful CMC environment is probably the key aspect in any online course.

I Devise a structure that meets the needs of the course and students

The CMC structure you devise will have a significant influence on how students use it. Before the course starts it is necessary to plan the structure so that the conferences will be used by students effectively, and that this usage corresponds with the educational objectives of the course. For instance, if you intend to have a collaborative exercise there may need to be a separate conference for this, to allow students to focus on the task related messages amidst the other communication. Conferences should avoid being 'in competition' with each other in terms of function. If you wish students to discuss the course material in their general student group conference, then do not create a separate conference for discussion. For general discussion, students will tend to migrate to the conference which offers the largest relevant audience. So, if there is more than one student group on a course, they will use the course-wide conference for discussion (but not a university-wide one). For specific activities with a defined goal they will work in smaller teams, either of the educator's choosing or their own selection. For such activities a large audience is not necessary; indeed, it is a distraction. The use of 'read-only' conferences and information resources also needs to be planned, so that students know where to find up-to-date course information, technical announcements, etc.

It is also important to decide whether you wish to incorporate 'chat' within the general conference or separate it out to a distinct conference. The access students have to non-course related conferences should also be considered. This can be at their own discretion, or the educator can decide which conferences are available to students on any one course. For example, students on a psychology course might have access to the university social conferences but also have an international conference on developmental psychology on their online desktops.

The issue of timing is also important. It may not be necessary to have all of the conferences available at the start of the course: rather, some can be introduced at appropriate stages in the course. Having a conference open before it is required may result in its being filled up with inappropriate messages before it is actually required.

2   Take advantage of the possibilities asynchronous communication offers

Asynchronous communication offers students a degree of flexibility over their study that is not possible in courses that are delivered face to face. This is a distinct advantage over conventional study methods and so should not be abandoned lightly. This liberation from time constraints may be more of a pull for students than the considerations of distance. In one study of distance education 95 per cent of students identified time constraints as a significant factor in not choosing face to face education (Hezel and Dirr, 1991). As my colleague Robin Mason puts it, 'time is the new distance':

> With the advent of telecommunications technologies, distance is less a barrier to education than it was before the networked personal computer. In fact, it is hardly an exaggeration to say that time is now the barrier that distance used to be in higher education.
>
> *(Mason and Weller, 2000)*

Asynchronous communication alleviates this pressure somewhat, in comparison with campus-based education. However, in comparison with traditional distance education courses, it introduces a degree of inflexibility and new time constraints, particularly when group work is used. Therefore a balance needs to be struck in any course between implementing elements that result in a loss of independence and working independently without the benefits of interaction. For this reason, activities which require synchronous communication should be used sparingly.

3 Appreciate the dynamic nature of courses with CMC

As I have argued, the student cohort has a strong influence in shaping the course environment through CMC. It might be argued that this is always the case with campus-based courses, but the extended time period for interactions exaggerates this influence in the online course. Cyberspace is a more malleable space than the physical one — it is what the users make it. Because the interactions take place over a more sustained time period, often involve more students than in a face to face situation, and crucially because the interaction *is* the course in many constructivist implementations, then the whole nature of a course can be determined by the manner in which students communicate. This leads to a somewhat worrying conclusion for distance educators — the course is never stable. What was a suitable conference structure for one cohort of students might not work for another set. An activity that was popular one year might not engage students the next.

In the first point I stressed the importance of establishing a conference structure that meets the course and student needs. This point adds the caveat — be prepared to change it. On T171 we have modified our conference structure on a yearly basis, in the light of student, tutor and moderator feedback. This has sometimes resulted in our reimplementing conferences that we had changed in the light of previous feedback. This is the nature of the beast: communication is a nebulous entity and the conditions it needs to flourish are not easily delineated. It will vary from student to student, as will the manner in which those students interact to create a course cohort with a personality of its own.

4 Develop a moderating style and guidelines

The nature of communication in an online environment is modified by the lack of visual cues, the prolonged timeframe of the dialogue and the anonymity afforded by the medium. This results in the need to develop online communication skills which will differ significantly from those used in everyday communication. Similarly, the skills required to teach online effectively need to be cultivated through experience and reflection. If you are new to online communication, valuable experience can be gained from simply observing a newsgroup, or preferably a variety of newsgroups, to appreciate different forms of behaviour.

As well as developing their own online style, it is important for educators and universities to establish a set of guidelines as to what constitutes acceptable (or perhaps more importantly, unacceptable) online behaviour. Students should be aware of a code of conduct to which they are agreeing by studying on a course. Many of the norms of behaviour that are easily established in a face to face situation can be seen by students online as a restriction of liberties. While no one would think it unusual to ask students to leave a lecture or tutorial if they were being disruptive or abusive, to remove a student from a conference is often interpreted as a free speech issue. Much of this attitude arises from the values inherent in the Net. It is seen as a vehicle of free speech, and many of the high-profile court cases have been about such issues. However, it is a mistaken belief that this means anyone can say what they like in any context. The Net is actually a place of incredible specialization. You can say (almost) anything you want, but in the right place. What is an acceptable posting in an adult humour conference is not acceptable in a children's conference, say. Students need to be made aware of the need to maintain a suitable educational environment from the outset. This can be done through a set of rules, but also by engaging the students and allowing them to determine a set of principles for their group conference, thus providing them with a sense of ownership over the online space.

Conclusion

In this chapter we have looked at the key features of online communication. One of the most significant of these is its asynchronous nature, which offers a number of potential benefits in education. Synchronous communication does have its uses and can often be used in conjunction with asynchronous. It does, however, result in a loss of flexibility.

The online environment will be determined by the types of conferences created, as well as the manner in which the student cohort uses them. Conferences can be used for a variety of functions on a course. It is important that students are clear with regards to the function of different conferences if they are to be used effectively. The learning objectives, scale and activities in a course will all have an influence on the types of conferences used.

Teaching via CMC requires the development of moderating skills that are different in nature or emphasis from those in face to face education. The social and dynamic nature of CMC driven courses result in an extended responsibility for the educator and different time considerations. Developing an approach to online teaching takes time and experience, and, above all, a willingness to learn and adapt.

In the next chapter we will look at how these issues and others associated with online education give rise to new working practices for educators.

Summary

In this chapter some of the issues relating to communication in online courses have been addressed. These were:

- differences from face to face communication;
- synchronous communication compared with asynchronous;
- types of computer conference;
- teaching via CMC, and the different requirements and issues associated with this medium.

From these issues four lessons for implementation were drawn:

● Devise a structure that meets the needs of the course and students.
● Take advantage of the possibilities asynchronous communication offers.
● Appreciate the dynamic nature of courses with CMC.
● Develop a moderating style and guidelines.

Chapter 7

New working methods

Introduction

As with any significant technology, the Net has an impact upon working practices. This has been seen in companies that have integrated the Internet and their own intranet into all aspects of corporate culture, for example Dell Computers, Cisco and Microsoft. As we saw earlier, e-commerce operations are developing new customer models and new working practices to accommodate the demands and the possibilities afforded by the new technologies. This has a knock-on effect for traditional retail outlets. In fact, the most interesting development of e-commerce may not be the rise of new online companies, but the changes it affects in existing companies. In order to compete with online operations which have increased richness and reach, traditional retail outlets have increased the profile of benefits they can offer, such as making shopping a more social experience, increased customer support, provision of other entertainment facilities in the same shopping area, and so forth.

The same trend may well be true in education. This is not to suggest that universities will be located next to funfairs, but rather that the impact of the Net will best be seen by observing the changes in working practice in established institutions.

In this chapter we will look at some of these possible changes and their implications for educators.

Team working

If you are producing an online course you now need to appreciate that you are an author and publisher. It is of course much easier to publish on the Web, but that ease can be a mixed blessing. The knowledge that something can be changed easily can lead to a rather casual attitude to publishing. For students, any ambiguity in material can be very confusing, resulting in wasted effort, discontentment and loss of confidence. On T171 one year, some students detected a slight ambiguity in an assignment question, despite its being checked by several authors and an editor (one needs to appreciate that some students can find ambiguity in almost any statement). Once it was raised in a conference a familiar 'snowballing of confusion' effect arose, so I decided to reword the assignment. This, however, led to the feeling that the Web site was not stable. As one student complained, 'It was changing on a daily basis!' Although only one alteration was made, it created the perception that the material was subject to change. In the light of this experience we now use the conference noticeboard (see previous chapter) to distribute any additional information, and avoid making changes to the Web site when possible.

Apart from being wary about altering Web sites, what this illustrates is the need to have others involved in the process of creating an online course. An editor or critical reader role is important for courses with a substantial Web site. Web education raises the profile of text for many educators who have previously relied on speech as their main mode of communication. The 'distance' aspect of the learning (even if students are not geographically distant) also requires that educators make their text clear, unambiguous and engaging. The fact that it can be changed easily should not be taken as an excuse not to expend energy in making the material suitable from the outset. As was suggested in Chapter 4, the Net makes everyone a distance educator, and this is one of the early lessons learnt by distance education establishments – the need to prepare carefully written material that acts as a teaching guide, compared with merely providing content in the form of books.

In addition, the educator may need to work with graphic designers. Having developed a number of Web sites, I appreciate that design is not one of my talents. Having seen a number of other Web sites developed by educators, I understand that I am not alone in this. Producing effective designs is a subtle skill, which the powerful Web site creation tools available can seduce you into thinking you possess. Do not be fooled. Students will be spending a lot of time in the Web environment of the course, and the look and feel of that space will have a strong effect on how they interact with it and how they perceive the course. The design and functionality of the online environment will have a similar effect on the student's learning experience to the physical architecture of a campus based university.

There are many Web sites specifying good design principles, so I will not elaborate on them here. Graphic designers will also often have a better appreciation of the types of design many students will be used to in external sites. The sort of students who are likely to study online are also likely to use the Net for many other activities, and so have a wide experience of different types of site. They will come to an online course with certain expectations about both functionality and design. A course that has a dated or poor design will create a bad impression regarding the educator or the institution. A site with confusing navigation and structure will have a detrimental effect on the student's interaction with the learning material.

Luckily, many course development environments (such as Web CT, Blackboard and Prometheus) have design templates available. In addition, any institution can develop its own set of templates. Through the use of technology such as XML (Extensible Markup Language, more of which later) or style sheets, the content of material and its design can be kept separate. Thus the author works in an environment which specifies the styles to be used, much like a word processor (in fact in some cases, a word processor is used), and then when the material is published, the software on the server combines the appropriate style sheets, producing a professional-looking Web page. This enables the author to quickly develop an online course, focusing mainly on the content.

In order to add richness to a course, educators may also need to work with programmers or Web developers to create animations, or databases, or sophisticated functionality within their Web site (for example, allowing students to create their own annotations on a Web site). It may also be necessary to liaise with those who run the Web servers, create and control conferences, and university Web administrators. Again, many of the course development environments incorporate tools to facilitate and automate many of these tasks.

The point here is that teaching is no longer a solitary pursuit. Whereas one educator could develop a lecture series, the online course requires collaboration with a range of individuals, the creation of teams. In producing its courses the OU has developed what it refers to as course teams, that is, multidisciplinary teams of authors, editors, graphic artists, video producers, software designers, course managers and so on. In 1976 Sir Walter Perry commented, 'The concept of the course team is, I believe, the most important single contribution of The Open University to teaching practice at tertiary level' (Perry, 1976: 91). In developing online courses many universities are establishing a form of the course team model, with educators working as part of a multidisciplinary team. The rise of online education may make Perry's remark even more salient.

Using the technology

It may seem an obvious thing to say, but in developing online courses, it pays to work in a manner which utilizes the technology to its fullest potential. The advantage of this is that one gains an appreciation of not only the technologies themselves, but also the culture associated with them. By culture I mean aspects such as the accepted tone for online communication, as well as appreciating the types of problems which arise, for instance compatibility of formats for file exchange, reaching consensus online, and so forth. If you are the type of person who prints out e-mails (or has your secretary print them out), then you simply will not engage with the subtle social elements of online behaviour that are only appreciated through exposure.

Working online also offers a number of benefits and opens up new methods for developing courses. The most obvious benefit is that just as students need not be tied to one location, neither do educators. Teleworking becomes more of a practical method of working, although it is not always to everyone's preference. As mentioned earlier, the potential for collaboration with academics from other universities is also enhanced. There are a number of software solutions (eg Groove, LotusNotes) which establish a joint working space, where documents can be shared, real-time and asynchronous interaction is supported, a variety of tools and templates are available for course development, and different working areas can be created. These can facilitate the team working approach stressed above, and remove the need for scheduling so many face to face meetings, which can act as a limiting factor in a group project.

Internet technologies can also lead to the development of working methods that were previously difficult, if not impossible, to realize. One such method is a database driven collection of 'learning objects' from which multiple courses can be created. There has been an increasing interest among some educators in the model of open source software movement and how it might be adapted to education. Open source software, such as Linux, is not developed by one company, as say Windows is by Microsoft. Instead it is developed by an open community of programmers. The code is freely available, and if there is a bug or an additional function that is required, then a programmer will develop a piece of code to achieve this and submit it to the group. If it is acceptable, then it is incorporated in the main code. The advantages of such an approach are:

- it spreads the complexity of software development across a wide number of developers (leading to more robust software, many argue);
- it is free and open, which matches the sensibilities of the Net;
- it can be updated very quickly, since it is not reliant on a major commercial release;
- it fosters a sense of community.

A similar approach in education might see a community of developers form around a particular topic, say the literature of Joseph Conrad (to choose an example which is definitely not related to the technology). Anyone can contribute to the database of learning objects. These can be anything: an article, a series of lectures in HTML, a PowerPoint presentation, an audio of a production of Conrad, images or whatever. Each object has a set of data (called meta-data since it is data about the data) associated with it that might indicate the level of the content, the title, language, learning outcomes, and so on. The learning objects would probably be 'vanilla' in style: that is, they have no design associated with them, so the user can incorporate his or her own design in to the course. As an educator I would then search the database for objects relating to the course I particularly want to develop, say on the novella *Heart of Darkness*, and aimed at first-year undergraduates. The sort of objects I might include would be:

- an annotated version of the text;
- articles on the symbolism in the book and the language;
- features and images of the Belgian Congo at the turn of the century;
- a brief biography of Conrad;
- an audio file of a production of *Heart of Darkness*.

Taking these objects I could add some elements of my own to create a cohesive course (I should then contribute these to the learning object pool for others to use). I can pass the unstyled contents through the university's own design templates, so I create a course with a cohesive look and feel, which is consistent with other offerings from the university. By adding and supporting my own assessment and exercises that encourage dialogue, interaction and participation, I create a unique course, even though many of its elements may be used in other courses.

This is part of a much larger movement in education to develop standards by which 'learning objects' can be specified, stored and reused. For example, the IMS project is a global consortium which is concerned with developing specifications 'for facilitating online distributed learning activities such as locating and using educational content, tracking learner progress, reporting learner performance, and exchanging student records between administrative systems' (http://www.imsproject.org/aboutims.html – December 2001). Similarly, the IEEE has instigated a Learning Standards Technology Committee which aims 'to develop Technical Standards, Recommended Practices, and Guides for software components, tools, technologies and design methods that facilitate the development, deployment, maintenance and interoperation of computer implementations of education and training components and systems' (http://ltsc.ieee.org – December 2001). Such approaches have the backing of many universities as well as commercial organizations such as Cisco and Microsoft. The key to such approaches is the development of learning objects: that is, modular building blocks which educators can use to construct a whole course.

There are a whole host of issues associated with such an approach, the most obvious of which concerns rights. By submitting material to such a pool the user is agreeing that it can be used freely by others. This in itself may be enough to put off some contributors, but, if successful, it does mean that education can become more accessible, which is in line with the core values of education itself. It may also be a fallacy that it is content that is important financially. MIT launched an initiative in 2001 called OpenCourseWare which makes its course notes, problems sets, quizzes and so on freely available on the Web. It suggests this is for altruistic reasons, but it also sends a very clear message – there is more to an MIT degree than just the content. It is the nature of the support, assessment and accreditation that is significant.

A full discussion of all the issues an open approach to content raises are beyond the scope of this book, but the important consideration here is that the Net facilitates new methods of working, which can substantially alter the way in which educators create and think about courses.

Elsewhere in the organization

A course does not exist in isolation. Universities and colleges have not only established a teaching approach based on the assumption of face to face contact, they have also developed a whole set of accompanying administrative procedures. The way in which students are assessed, how they interact with the organization of the university, how they receive information and the facilities to which they have access are all determined by the underlying assumption of physical colocation. Once this assumption is removed, the processes that have been developed to achieve these functions in this manner might no longer be suitable. For the educator this means that many of the general support processes which they could previously take for granted could no longer apply. The educator then has to liaise with other sections of the university to develop new procedures or adapt existing ones. This is particularly true for early adopters of the technology. It is exacerbated by the tendency for educators who are developing online courses to want to innovate in a number of areas, such as assessment and resources. It is important to ensure that the online students are not disadvantaged in any way, so equivalents for all the information, support and resources available to campus based students need to be established. Educators can then find their energies being directed into creating a whole support structure and gaining an encyclopaedic knowledge of university regulations. Being an online educator is liable to bring you into contact with other parts of the university in new ways and with a different set of questions.

There are several areas which impact directly on a course, and it is therefore worth investigating how the online course will be affected by these. The first of these is exams and assessment. We will look at assessment in detail in the next chapter, but for now it is important to appreciate that the assessment of online courses may take a different form, complete with its own problems, from conventional assessment. The first casualty of the online course is often the traditional exam, to be replaced by a project or some form of end of course assessment. If this is the case, does the university have procedures for dealing with issues of verification for distance students?

This has always been a problem in distance education, which was initially solved by holding conventional exams in distributed regions with a proof of identity burden on the students. Replacing exams with projects has led to the development of procedures such as verification by the tutor that this is the student's work, random selection for telephone vivas, automatic checks for plagiarism and so forth. All of these work to create a reasonable deterrent to cheating. However, if the exams and assessment department in a university is unaccustomed to distance students, and treats the conventional exam as the norm, then the online educator will have to develop procedures to satisfy the quality assurance demands. As with any new approach, it is often the case that these are more stringent and demanding than existing ones, to ensure quality is maintained and to defend against possible criticism.

Another area that will impact upon the online course is that of technical support. I have already stressed the importance of working as part of a team with technical expertise during the development of a course. During the presentation of a course this support is also vitally important. First of all, it is necessary to ascertain whether the software you are using on a course is supported. If you have decided to use a favourite package of your own, then it may not be, so any problems you, or the students, might have will need to be solved on your own. Any online course creates a technical barrier for students, even if they are advanced students attempting to do sophisticated tasks with the software. The issue of technical support for students is therefore always going to be a pertinent one. For this reason it is easier to fall in with whatever software the university has standardized upon, even if you feel it is not the best option. Alternatively, you can arrange support yourself. The degree of support for online students will vary depending on the university. Is there a helpdesk available? What hours is it staffed (remember online students will work at unconventional hours)? Are the helpdesk staff familiar with your course and the software it uses? These are all questions that the online educator may need to address.

You may feel that by using a standard Web browser for delivery and conferencing, with common plug-ins such as Macromedia Flash for animation, then the need for support is minimal. While it is true that browsers are reasonably robust, and many have inbuilt plug-in capability, there will always be students who raise questions, or who have specific technical difficulties. One student will want to know if he can run the software on a Linux system while another will ask why whenever she logs in the system crashes, and so forth. If a central support area can deal with such queries, then it can save a lot of time for educators who may not have sufficient knowledge to answer such queries. It also helps students in having one central area to ask such queries, where they will often find a set of Frequently Asked Questions (FAQs) which deal with them. Many of the companies offering the course development systems mentioned above will provide this technical support facility for students.

Often such areas will overlap: for instance, if students are submitting assignments electronically, does the exams and assessment department want these to be submitted to a central system, or direct to the educator? The former method allows tracking and logging of assessment, in the case of appeals and for recording purposes. It requires a complex system to be developed, however, whereas the second option can be accomplished via e-mail; but this may leave the educator exposed. For instance, what if a student subsequently changes and improves the assignment and then appeals against the mark he or she has been awarded? Can the educator prove it has been altered after it was marked? Such proof is easier with a central system. However, a central system leads to a loss of flexibility, so the technical support staff will need to advise educators on potential problems with submissions, limitations of the system, and so on. In such situations educators can find themselves caught between the rock of assessment regulations and the hard place of technical feasibility.

Another area that will impact upon students is access to resources, for example the library. For online students this may be less of an issue, since they can have access to a wide range of resources. However, libraries are undergoing a fundamental change in their mode of operation, brought about by information and communication technologies (ICT). It is worth establishing with the library what facilities they can offer distance students, for example access to databases, online journals, book loans and remote access to CD ROMs. In addition, the library staff will often be willing to help in developing new services which could be beneficial to the course.

Lastly, one area of the university that will impact upon the educator in particular is that of university management and administration. Online courses have different demands and requirements that managers need to be aware of. For instance, it is easy to monitor workload for face to face lectures (it is very obvious if someone fails to turn up), but this is less obvious for online courses which are more distributed over time. The tracking and recording of online activities means that in some respects more information is available, but it will be a different type of activity. The time demands of online teaching need to be appreciated if educators are not to be overloaded. The practices of education have been established on the assumption of face to face contact, and so the evidence of work is related to physical presence. The online educator raises a number of questions for university management such as:

- Is the university happy for educators to work at home? For an online course this may be a more effective working environment than an office.
- Is the university willing to provide equipment for teleworkers?
- Does teleworking lessen the recognition or promotion prospects of an individual?
- Are other work commitments taken away from educators in order to give them time to develop online courses and skills, or is this development an additional burden?
- Is there appropriate staff development in place?
- Does the course fulfil part of the university's overall Internet strategy (if one exists)?
- Does the educator have the backing of senior management in implementing necessary changes to procedures?

If the answer to any of these questions is 'no', then the university as a whole must question its commitment to online learning, and the success of any such venture is unlikely on any large scale.

Using the technology within the organization

Combining the previous two sections, another way in which the Net will affect methods of working will be in the integration of the technology within the organization. While many companies, institutions and universities have a strong external Internet presence, internally they still rely on standard methods, for example using paper forms for expenses, memos for information, handbooks for staff resources and so on.

Most large organizations have begun to use an intranet, which utilizes Web technology to create an internal network which can only be accessed by staff. This can be a useful way of archiving information, so that staff can access information such as policies, forms and papers. However, the effort is often rather half-hearted, and the online documentation incomplete. Even when the archiving is good, it is something of a façade: the actual processes which underlie the documentation are not facilitated by the technology. For example, one might be able to locate an expenses form online, and find the appropriate rates and advice on completion, but the form still needs to be printed out and posted to senior management for approval, from where it is sent to accounts to deal with, and so on. A truly online organization would have a form which is completed online, which automatically sends a summary e-mail to the senior management, and at the same time arranges for automatic transfer of money to the claimant's account. The manager need do nothing unless he or she wishes to prevent the payment.

Much of the administrative workload in large organizations can be automated. It often remains time-consuming and expensive because it is based on the handling of physical paper. By utilizing the technology to its full potential it is possible to alleviate some of the administrative burden facing educators and make significant savings. This is usually only achievable through top-down directives and some initial heavy investment into the appropriate systems.

Bill Gates explains how he first realized the problem of paper forms:

In 1996 I decided to look into the ways that Microsoft, a big advocate of replacing paper with electronic forms, was still using paper. To my surprise, we had printed 350,000 paper copies of sales reports that year. I asked for a copy of every paper form we used. The thick binder that landed on my desk contained hundreds and hundreds of forms...

I looked at this binder of forms and wondered, 'Why do we have all of these forms? Everybody here has a PC. We're connected up. Why aren't we using electronic forms and e-mail to streamline our processes and replace all this paper?'

Well, I exercised the privilege of my job and banned all unnecessary forms. In place of all that paper, systems grew up that were far more accurate and far easier to work with and that empowered our people to do more interesting work.

(Gates, 1999: 40)

He then goes on to give a practical example of how it works at Microsoft, relating to the hiring of a new employee, Sharon:

Before Sharon arrives at Microsoft, an administrative assistant in her new group fills out the electronic New Hire Setup form in Microsoft's intranet to request a voice-mail account, an e-mail account, office furniture, and a computer with preinstalled software to be ready on Sharon's arrival. The same form ensures that Sharon gets added to the company phone-list, receives a nameplate for her office door, and gets a mailbox in her building's mailroom. The single electronic form goes directly to the groups responsible for taking care of these items. Electronic logs ensure that everything is tracked.

... Sharon and the other new employees are directed to the company's internal Web site for most of their administrative needs. Sharon goes online to review the employee handbook (it no longer exists in paper form), download any software she needs beyond the standard setup, and fill out her electronic W-4 form.

Next Sharon uses a procurement tool on our intranet called MS Market to order office supplies, books, a whiteboard and business cards. MS Market automatically fills in her name, her e-mail alias, the name of her approving manager, and other standard information for the order... An order above a certain amount of money requires additional levels of management approval before processing. Our electronic system routes the form to the right people for an electronic okay.

And so on, including signing up for journals, bulletins, booking travel, and managing stock options. Other companies, such as Cisco, have also reported how they have used similar systems to reduce or eliminate paper forms and dramatically cut costs and administrative overheads. Since it is a 'knowledge' industry there are many ways in which similar approaches could benefit those in education, but few universities or colleges would be able to lay claim to such an integrated system.

If a university is to really become a major provider of online courses, then it should utilize the technology to change its own working practices also. Failure to do so means that it might not be able to compete with the commercial organizations that do adopt such an approach. It can also result in not fully realizing the potential of the technology. Successful online organizations such as Amazon and Cisco integrate the technology throughout their working practice. This is not just because they believe that it offers practical benefits, but also because in so doing they foster an 'Internet' culture. It is true that the Net is just a technology, but it is also a space, an environment and it has its own set of cultural values. Nicholas Negroponte (1996) makes the distinction between atoms and bits, and each can be said to have its own set of rules and behaviour. Physical objects, for instance, are expensive to reproduce, whereas digital objects are virtually free. Much of the difficulty in shifting from a physical based approach to an online one arises from this tension between the culture of atoms and the culture of bits. It can be manifest in subtle, but nonetheless obstinate ways.

For example, in 1996 I initiated an electronic tutor group on a different OU course (Weller, 2000a), which otherwise had the standard face to face tutorial model. It was a tremendously time-consuming task to realize, because the existing administrative structures were based on a face to face model. For instance, a tutor is usually appointed in the same geographical region as the student (for administrative purposes the OU divides the UK into 13 separate geographical regions). Consequently, systems have been devised whereby the money associated with each student is allocated to the appropriate region and the general support for tutors and students is the responsibility of the region. Having students from all over the country allocated to one tutor proved difficult to organize within this structure. Similarly, the tutor contract was based on the number of face to face tutorials the tutor gave. Whereas tutorials represent a single entity, so they can be paid on an hourly basis, online tutoring is more distributed over time and did not match easily on to the tutor contract. And so on. The OU has now addressed many of these issues at a university level as more courses have adopted such approaches. The difficulties arose, however, through the mismatch in cultures, and often the solutions developed were a case of trying to fit the online model into existing structures; the fit was not always an easy one. This may not represent a long-term solution, however, and only organizations that really take the Net to the heart of their working life will develop the appropriate procedures and methodologies.

New problems

Any new way of working inevitably brings its own set of problems and issues. An Internet enhanced working practice has its fair share of these. I will summarize what I feel are the six main areas of concern for online educators.

Workload

A case has been made for how ICT can be used to lighten some workload, but the opposite is also true. Online courses that make heavy use of asynchronous communication do not have the natural boundaries found in conventional lecture-based education. Lectures and tutorials occupy a specific time slot, with perhaps informal drop-in sessions afterwards. The great advantage of online education for students is its anytime, anyplace aspect. This can be one of the disadvantages for the educator, however. Teaching can easily bleed into home life, evenings and weekends. How often should you be online? How soon should students expect a response? Should you respond to all messages? Conscientious educators can often be responsible for their own downfall, feeling they just have to have one more look. I remember posting responses to queries, then checking repeatedly to see if the student had read or responded to it, often to the detriment of other work. Similarly, I used to be online regularly over the weekend, so that when Friday came, it did not feel as though work had finished.

One can develop coping mechanisms, however. As mentioned in the previous chapter, it is not always beneficial to respond to every message, since this can discourage other students from contributing. There will, of course, be messages to which you have to respond, but for others it may be advantageous for all to encourage a student response first. The workload issue can also be addressed by setting clear boundaries and expectations for students. For instance, you might state at the beginning of the course that you will be online three times a week, giving set days. Students then know they will receive a response by these days, and if the issue is urgent they can telephone. You may well check messages more frequently than this, but it sets a level of expectation which is manageable with other demands.

Information overload

This is an overused term but, for anyone who uses e-mail intensively and returns from a week's holiday, a familiar feeling. As with workload, the benefit of e-mail is also its problem. It is very easy to send, so one's mailbox quickly fills up with junk mail, messages that have been copied to everyone, replies to these messages, requests, comments, and so on. In addition there are a number of conferences that need looking at, and soon one feels that it is impossible to catch up. On returning from a two-week holiday once I estimated that with my different e-mail accounts and numerous student and staff conferences to look into I had something in the region of 500 messages to read. Of course, one becomes selective then and can ignore whole threads or discussions, but nevertheless it was a daunting prospect.

This is the key to dealing with information overload – being selective. In my first flushes of enthusiasm for the Net I signed up for a whole range of discussion lists. I quickly learnt that I was simply deleting most of the messages from these, and unsubscribed. I also delete messages into which I am copied but which are irrelevant to me, and automatically delete any replies to this, since they arise from people using reply-all rather than reply-sender (one of my pet hates!). I can also dip into many conferences to gain a flavour of them without reading every message.

Systems that help in filtering queries or devolving responsibility can also drastically reduce the number of messages one needs to read. For example, we have developed a conferencing structure for T171 that has moderators for every conference, and each moderator has access to a higher-level conference, where he or she can bring any issues. Therefore it is important to read this higher-level conference, and respond to queries, but the others can be entrusted to the moderators. If you implement a rota system for responsibility for the higher-level conference, the workload can be split across a number of individuals.

Other techniques include limiting the time you read e-mails, for instance checking once in the morning, then at lunchtime. By not having the e-mail package open continuously one can focus on other work. I must confess that I do have my e-mail open all the time, since I like to deal with messages as they arrive, but it can be distracting.

Stress

Working and teaching online brings its own set of challenges and problems, which can create stress. One aspect peculiar to this mode of working is the extended argument or disagreement. The asynchronous nature of communication means that an exchange extends over several days. This can be beneficial in that it allows one time to compose replies, but it can also lead to stress, since a confrontation, disagreement or problem becomes extended. Many educators I have spoken to have reported the phenomenon of mentally composing e-mail replies at 4 am. Whereas a face to face confrontation is limited in time, the online one can linger, since there is always more to add, creating a very stressful situation if you are caught up in such a disagreement. Even if the discussion is not disagreeable, one is still involved in several different conversations at the same time, all stretching over a prolonged period. Being always in the middle of different conversations can be a mentally exhausting task.

Related to the problem of lengthy disagreements is the nature of communication e-mail often engenders. The ease with which a message can be sent, combined with the relative anonymity mentioned earlier, makes it an ideal medium for complaining or airing grievances. Thus educators may find the number of complaints they deal with increases when compared with face to face teaching. This is not necessarily a result of increased dissatisfaction, but rather a result of lowering the threshold for complaint. To criticize a lecturer face to face is a socially inhibiting situation for many students, but they can easily send an e-mail. Also, the ease with which e-mail can be sent means students can complain at the time they are feeling frustrated, for example while they are doing an assignment. Such complaints may well be valid and perhaps encouraged, but education necessarily requires learners to work hard and struggle with the process if they are to really learn anything. Often students can only appreciate the point of exercises or assignments after the fact. Another related issue is that it only takes a few vocal students to generate a lot of messages, which can give the appearance that everyone is dissatisfied. In the pilot year of T171 one conference seemed to be full of complaints, but when we conducted a course survey over 80 per cent of students indicated that they were enjoying the course, and many stated that they felt intimidated by the vocal students in the conference. The impression gained from the conference was not representative of the whole.

This stress is increased by the additional responsibility the online educator has for the educational environment, which I touched upon in the previous chapter. The asynchronous communication and integration of social aspects into the learning environment broaden the type of interaction that occurs. The educator has to ensure that a suitable environment is maintained without being heavy-handed. This can involve the educator being pulled into disagreements between students, dealing with possible harassment, interpreting what constitutes offence to one party and so forth. All of this can cause additional anxiety.

One only really learns to deal with such issues through experience. It is important to establish the right tone early on in a conference. If students feel the educator is working with them they are less likely to be confrontational. Similarly, if the group bonds well then disapproval by peers can become a deterrent to anti-social behaviour. Establishing acceptable communication and behavioural guidelines can also help students themselves maintain a suitable environment.

Technology churn

Once you enter the online world, you step onto a treadmill for, as we are all aware, ICT is in a constant state of change. What was acceptable one year looks dated the next. Functions you achieved through clumsy methods can now be achieved easily with new software. Students have experienced more advanced technology on other Web sites and expect it in the course.

Keeping up to date is a difficult and time-consuming task. How far should one go? If the Net is to be a widespread educational technology, then it must be easy to use. Educators are busy enough with teaching and trying to stay current in their particular field without having to be experts in Internet technologies. On the other hand, there is the demand from online students for educational sites to be comparable in functionality and quality to other sites with which they are familiar. The changes in technology often introduce new functions, which means the educator can realize tasks that were difficult to achieve previously.

One means of at least being familiar with current developments is to integrate the Net into your working practice, as I have suggested above. If using the Net is something additional, then trying to catch up on developments once a year becomes an arduous task, whereas if you use it intensively for all aspects of work, then you develop an appreciation of developments almost by osmosis.

The importance of team working and developing a good network of people who can explain the latest developments is essential if the stress caused by technology churn is to be alleviated. Having people of whom you can reliably ask questions, or access to a series of seminars where such developments are explained and demonstrated, is essential. It is not the case that educators themselves need be expert in using the development tools, but they should know what those tools can do. With much of the Net it is not a matter of being able to perform a task yourself, but rather of knowing to ask for it that is significant. XML is a good example of this. You need not know how to implement XML in detail, but an appreciation of what it means for an online course is important if you are to use it to its potential. I will look at this in more detail in a later chapter.

Intrusion

This is really a much broader issue than education, and applies to all uses of the Net. The fact is that by working online there is the potential for senior management to gather a lot of information. For instance, the Web sites you visit, when you last checked a conference, how long you were online for, the content of all your e-mails and so on are all pieces of information which are relatively easy to gather technically, although there are regulations about doing so. The ability to be able to gather this information is sometimes irresistible for senior managers. In her book *Close to the Machine*, Ellen Ullman (1997) gives the following account of a conversation with a manager (whom she refers to as 'William Banner') for whom she has just installed a new office network system:

Mr. Banner leaned over to me and asked, 'Can you keep track of keystrokes?'
… 'Keystrokes?' I asked.
'You know, on the computer. The keys. Can you keep a record of every key someone enters?'
… 'Well, yes. You could. Yes, there are ways to do that.'
'What would it cost to do it?'
'To keep keystrokes? I don't know offhand. But why? Why would you want to do that?'
… 'Well, take Mary. I'd like to know everything that Mary does in a day.'
Mary was the receptionist and general office manager. She was William Banner's oldest employee, twenty-six years. As I recalled, Mary knew every one of the company's clients by name. For the first several years of her employment, when Mr. Banner's kids were small, she used to pick them up from school, take them home, and pour them milk.
'But why do you want to keep an eye on Mary? She's doing very well with the system. I mean, is there a problem?'
'Oh, no. No problem,' said William Banner, 'but, you know… Well I'm curious. All those years she's been out there running things, and now I can find out exactly what she does.'
'So you want to know about Mary just because you can?' I asked.
… 'Hmm. That's it, I suppose.'

Whilst few in an educational establishment would want to emulate Mr. Banner, the 'because you can' factor is always difficult to resist. And collecting much of that data is easier now everyone is online.

It does not matter if someone is actually collecting all this information for it to be a cause of anxiety. What matters to many people is that someone *could*. Governments, companies and universities are all developing regulations to control this, but in the broader context there are many cases which are testing the law and how it should be applied to the Internet. It is worth ensuring that you are familiar with the regulations laid down by your organization and being cautious about what you send or look at over the Net from university machines. While everyone may agree that people should not be using university machines to access certain types of Web sites (or that some perhaps should not be viewable at all), legislation can be clumsier than this.

Social life

As we saw in Chapter 2, the social aspect of university study is an important motivational factor for students. This applies to educators also. Employment fulfils a social role as well as an economic one. If there is a shift to increasingly working online and doing this from the home, the opportunity for this social contact may be lessened. Any organization acts as a conduit for social interaction through canteens, informal meetings in corridors, events such as birthdays, formal meetings, and so on. The effect of these interactions is often subtle and unquantifiable, but they can perform all or some of the following functions:

● increase a person's sense of belonging to the organization;
● lead to the development of new ideas or projects;
● expand knowledge;
● provide enjoyment;
● increase job satisfaction.

Therefore anything which affects this delicate and complex set of interactions could have unforeseen circumstances for both the employee and the organization. Employees may feel isolated, or may just find they lack motivation. The organization may find it has increased productivity, but less innovation, say.

This is one of the reasons many people choose not to opt for complete teleworking, but rather maintain an 'office presence', while taking advantage of the possibilities for teleworking on a regular basis, as tasks demand.

Working online can, of course, open up new connections and one can develop new friendships and networks. If you are teleworking a great deal, then establishing this sort of online network of formal and informal dialogues is important to realize many of the functions outlined above (although such networks are likely to extend beyond the organization).

The flipside to the loss of socialization at work is the impact of work on one's home life. In a recent survey reported in an article entitled 'Fears over long hours hamper teleworking take-up' in *ZDNet*, 30 July 2001, 84 per cent of UK managers said they expected to be in 'office mode' for longer hours if they worked from home. As I mentioned above, this feeling that you can always check e-mail, or that you are involved in an ongoing discussion, can make it difficult to draw boundaries between home and work.

Developing such boundaries and creating new forms of social interaction is something that is likely to evolve as working online becomes increasingly commonplace in employment. The Internet is a communication technology after all, so if we are aware that socialization is a significant factor in employment, then people will find ways to realize it through new technologies as well as face to face.

Lessons for implementation

1   Rethink working practice

This applies to organizations as a whole as well as individual educators. The need to rethink almost every aspect of educational work lies at the heart of success online. Educators need to develop new ways of creating courses, address the need for new roles in this process, find different methods of assessment, look at alterations in support mechanisms and be aware of new demands on the university. The organization needs to develop administrative, quality control, financial and support procedures that meet the needs of online students and educators.

This can seem such a daunting task that it makes one question the desire to provide online education at all. It is important to realize that the existing methods and procedures did not exist in some Platonic sense. They have evolved over time. The same will happen with the necessary online procedures. The actual content and form of these will only become apparent through experience, and will vary from institution to institution. Some will find that simply adapting existing methodologies will be acceptable, whereas others feel that a completely different set of procedures will be necessitated. The important issue is that having all of these systems in place is not the *sine qua non* for implementing an online course. Rather, it should be appreciated that they will need addressing, and individuals and organizations will need to maintain the awareness and flexibility to do so.

2   Develop coping mechanisms

Any substantial change in working practice brings with it anxiety (as well as excitement). In order to deal with anxiety and related stress, and also to be an effective online educator, one needs to develop new methods for coping with these and related issues. I have suggested some of these above, including working as part of a team, developing a support network, setting reasonable expectations and work limits, and so on.

We have become so accustomed to the face to face assumption in education that we do not appreciate how many of these coping mechanisms have been developed over the years. For example, specifying hours when you are available for student consultation, having allocated time for research or even teaching via set books can all be viewed as means of coping with the demands of face to face education. Working online brings with it a new, or at least altered, set of demands. Developing the appropriate working practices to deal with these is likely to take time, so one should initially be prepared for an increase in workload and maybe stress as these practices evolve.

3   Integrate the technology

This again applies both at the individual and organizational level. By integrating the technology into everyday working practice the educator gains a sensitivity and awareness to the associated issues. This can mean working as part of a distributed team, using the Net for research, engaging in discussion fora, and so forth. For the organization the need to integrate the technology throughout the administrative, staff and financial processes relates not only to potential savings but also to the development of a Net culture. This will make the organization as a whole better equipped to deal with the demands of online students and educators.

Conclusion

The new methods of working facilitated or necessitated by the technology have been addressed above. These include the need to develop appropriate teams for course development and presentation, and the potential the technology offers for new methods of course creation. Within the organization the online course will create different demands in a number of different areas, which the educator and management need to address. As well as offering a potential for new ways of working more efficiently, the Net also brings a host of potential problems for educators and universities. Addressing issues relating to educator working practices and related stress may well be the deciding factor in the success of online education in any one university.

The significance of assessment has been mentioned in terms of both the pedagogy of a course and the administrative support necessary for innovation. Assessment is often the area where innovation, technology and pedagogy combine to the greatest effect for students, educators and universities. This is what we will look at in the next chapter.

Summary

In this chapter several issues relating to changes in working practice for educators have been raised. These are brought about by the demands of delivering online courses and also the possibilities the technology creates. The issues are:

- the need to work in teams when developing online courses;
- using the technology to develop courses: for example, adapting the open source approach;
- looking at the impact elsewhere in the organization: for example, the areas of exams and assessment, technical support, management and administration;
- making effective use of the technology within the organization;
- new problems caused by this way of working, including issues such as workload, information overload, stress, technology churn, intrusion and changes in social aspects of working life.

Three lessons for implementation were drawn from these issues:

- Rethink working practice.
- Develop coping mechanisms.
- Integrate the technology.

Chapter 8

Assessment

Introduction

For many students, assessment *is* the course, and success in assessment is their ultimate goal. For educators it represents the means by which they can determine how much of the course students have really learnt, and measure the progress of students. For universities, accrediting courses, maintaining assessment standards and safeguarding against cheating represent some of the key roles and responsibilities of the institution. It is therefore unsurprising that it is in the area of assessment that many of the changes wrought by online education will be felt most keenly.

If an online course brings about a change in pedagogy, use of new technology and even different academic content, then it follows that new methods of assessment are likely to be required. In this chapter some of the ways in which assessment can be used online and also some of the issues surrounding it will be addressed.

Assessing group work

The increased use of collaborative and cooperative work in online courses raises a number of assessment related issues. If the educator wants students to engage in the collaborative process and give it the attention it requires, then it needs to be linked to the formal assessment of the course. Even if students find group work beneficial, enjoyable and rewarding, there is always a temptation to focus on activities that relate directly to assessment. Given the time and energy it requires to achieve successful group working, it is likely to be one of the first elements to be dropped strategically by students if they begin to feel the pressure of study and it is not related to assessment. The ways in which it can be linked to assessment are varied, and relate to the amount of credit given for individual and group elements, the pedagogy of the course and the degree to which the process rather than the outcome is included in the assessment.

This last factor demonstrates one of the ways in which the online course allows different elements to be included in assessment. The asynchronous and self-documenting quality of the interaction in online courses opens up the possibility of allocating marks for contribution to the process itself, rather than basing it solely on outcome. This is particularly relevant in group work, where some individuals may contribute to the group exercise more than others. One of the common complaints relating to assessed group work is that it benefits lazy students, since they can get a 'free ride' if one mark is awarded to the overall group outcome. By allocating a proportion of the marks to the quality of the individual contribution to the process this can be alleviated. It also has strong pedagogic validity, since it emphasizes the importance of participation in the learning process.

A similar balance can be achieved by devising a group task which has an overall group element, but also an individual contribution: for example, a Web site where each individual is responsible for one page and collectively the students are responsible for the index page and the overall design. This allows the assessment to distinguish between individual and group elements, while maintaining a strong collaborative emphasis.

Assessment can also relate to group work less directly. For instance, a collaborative exercise can be implemented, and the assessment specify that students reflect, comment on or analyse how the group process worked, according to specified criteria. Such a method means that even if a group does not work well, the students can still complete the assessment.

Some educators allocate marks for contribution to the discussion in a course which is not necessarily related to a specific group activity, but they make general contribution a mandatory requirement for passing the course. This sends a clear message that participation is expected, but unless marks are awarded for the content of messages, it can lead to students sending messages simply to meet the criteria, which add nothing to the discussion.

In all assessment of group work a careful balance needs to be maintained between encouraging participation in the activity and punishing individual students because of the activities (or often, inactivity) of others.

Exams and projects

The traditional exam is a convention that was designed to meet certain needs and offer particular advantages. When all the students are based on campus, it offers a convenient one-off test that can remove doubts about collusion. There have long been complaints associated with the conventional exam, in that it represents an unfair test that can be influenced by factors on a specific day, it may benefit certain individuals with an aptitude for tests, and it does not really demonstrate a student's understanding of a subject, but rather their ability to pass exams. There has been an increase in the number of courses which adopt a project-type assessment or some form of continual assessment in order to address some of these issues and provide students with a range of assessment experiences. Online courses, particularly those that adopt a constructivist approach, place a strong emphasis on interaction, communication and the individual's development of concepts. The traditional exam is not only unsuitable for such courses, but is directly opposed to many of the underlying educational objectives of the course.

This means such courses need to find new forms of assessment that meet the demands and objectives of the course, while also satisfying the criteria for assessment that the university stipulates. One of the benefits of the traditional exam was that it provided students with a definite culmination to a course, which was somewhat cathartic. It also provides an opportunity for synthesis, so students could bring together the different elements they had learnt during the course and see the connecting themes, rather than viewing them as separate, linear pieces of information. There is some value, then, in having some form of end of course assessment and not just continual assessment. If the issues mentioned above in group work are addressed, then the group component can form the overall assessment for a course and meet these needs. Other approaches, which we will look at below, include portfolio and reflection based assessment. These allow the student to be assessed fairly on work throughout the course, while providing room for individual expression and synthesis.

Automatic assessment

For many people, when they think of assessment in online courses, they assume that what is meant is some form of automated assessment. Much of this is born from a view that the Web is a multi-media delivery system. The emphasis in such a view is on developing virtual tools to aid learning and to engage the students. This can make the material more motivating for students and promote deeper learning through interaction.

The most obvious form of automatic assessment is the multiple choice quiz. Most course development software has the capability for generating multiple choice quizzes, so they can be implemented easily by the educator. By providing feedback on correct and incorrect answers they can be used during the course to correct common misconceptions. If they are used in formal assessment, then some of their learning value can be diminished, since students do not get the chance to repeatedly take the test and learn from their mistakes. Although multiple choice quizzes can be useful for students to test their understanding of concepts, and they add some variety to a Web site, their use in testing or promoting deeper understanding is limited.

Automatic assessment can be extended beyond the standard multiple choice quiz using some imagination and flexible software such as Macromedia Flash or Java applets. For instance, students can be asked to complete equations or answer questions in a free text input. A range of acceptable answers can be programmed and common incorrect answers can be incorporated with appropriate feedback. The removal of a range of answers means students have to think harder about the answer, rather than simply spotting the right answer in the selection.

Other variations on automatic assessment can involve more game-like activities. Here are some examples:

- Students can be required to sort objects or concepts into categories by dragging and dropping the object.
- A graph is completed by students to indicate what would occur after a certain event.
- A compound object such as a sentence, chemical, film scene, etc is decomposed into its elements by the student.
- A timeline is created by students adding predetermined events.
- In a game students have to place falling concepts into the correct containers.

Many of these add an element of fun and interactivity to a course. In creating activities which incorporate an element of game play the educator needs to strike a balance between making the activity interesting and engaging, and allowing these elements to overshadow the educational objectives of the activity. As with multiple choice, these forms of assessment are usually better suited to self-testing, rather than constituting part of the formal assessment on a course. If students are allowed to engage with them repeatedly, free from the pressures and constraints of formal assessment, they can be a useful means of reinforcing concepts.

More sophisticated approaches have been developed which allow automatic assessment of essays (eg Foltz, Laham and Landauer, 1999; Shermis *et al*, 2001). This software works by creating a semantic map for an answer and then assessing the 'distance' of an essay from that answer. The semantic map can be created by feeding the software with course texts or model answers. The correlation of such software with human markers is reportedly high, making it a reliable method. It can provide detailed feedback in terms of content and style to the student. It can also identify plagiarism reliably. As with quizzes, automatic essay marking is perhaps better suited as a tool for student self-improvement rather than as a means of automatically assessing course work.

Such software does demonstrate the potential for automatic assessment. As such approaches become more sophisticated, their integration into online courses will become increasingly useful. However, whether automatic assessment for a whole course would be acceptable to students is a debatable issue. For some courses, particularly those in the Web based training (WBT) domain, such assessment may

well be acceptable to gain a certificate of completion. For university level education it is unlikely that students would want their education to be so devoid of
human contact. In addition, a course that adopts a constructivist pedagogy will
find that such assessment does not suit the approach and the course aims.

This role of automatic assessment is a supportive one to the overall assessment
in the course. Some form of automated test can be included in the formal aspect,
but it is unlikely to constitute the whole assessment for university level education.
Commercial training and general interest courses may well be served by such
assessment. Its greatest benefit in a course is to provide a means of promoting
interactivity and allowing self-assessment.

Other types of online assessment

The use of different teaching approaches has caused many educators who have
implemented online courses to search for different forms of assessment from the
traditional exam or essay. This has occurred within a much broader shift in the
view of assessment and criticism of current assessment methods. Boud (1988), for
instance, argues that conventional assessment techniques are not consistent with
some goals of education, such as developing independent learners and critical
thinkers. Similarly, Hodgkinson and Dillon (2001) suggest that traditional assessment methods do not sit easily with the move to the development of key skills in
curricula. Online courses have therefore adopted and adapted many practices that
have been implemented in other campus based or distance education courses.
Some of these approaches are outlined here, although the coverage is by no
means exhaustive, and often a combination of the methods here can be used.

The Web as resource

Such an approach encourages students to take advantage of the Web as a vast
resource. This encourages them in online research, provides an opportunity to
analyse a range of material, gives exposure to different views, makes the assessment more active and requires interpretation of a wide scope of material within a
given framework. Such an approach can be realized in a variety of ways, such as:

● a conventional essay with marks allocated to the use of the Web as a resource;
● a group project with each member contributing one or more sites;
● an exercise in information skills, whereby students find, evaluate and summarize a specified number of sites on a given topic;
● problem based, whereby students have to find the necessary information to
  solve a set task.

Such an approach can be time-consuming for students, so adequate accommoda-
tion for this needs to be built in to the course by the educator. There is also an

issue about the reliability of information found on the Web, but being able to evaluate such information is an important skill, so this represents a useful teaching opportunity. Other advantages for both educator and students of such an approach include:

- It ensures the course is up to date, since the Web will contain the most current information.
- It lessens some of the need for the course itself to carry all information.
- It provides a form of legitimate peripheral participation, since the students are engaged in a research-type activity.
- It facilitates dialogue between students and the educator as they discuss sites.
- It encourages the view of educator as co-participant, since the students are likely to find sites that are unfamiliar to the educator.

New student roles

Just as online courses have often seen a change in the student role in learning, so the use of assessment in online courses can see students taking a more active role in the assessment process. By doing so students feel a greater sense of ownership over the assessment process, but there are a significant number of potential pitfalls.

One way in which students can become more actively involved in the assessment process is through peer evaluation. When students have worked in groups they can award each other a mark for their contributions. These peer scores form a part of the overall score: for example, 10 per cent may be formed from the average of the peer scores (eg Earl, 1986). The potential problems with such an approach are that personal feelings can influence the scores, that marks are given according to personality rather than contribution, that it creates a stressful situation for students, that it can lead to group disharmony and that it raises questions about the validity of the marks. It does, however, encourage students to participate in the group process and makes them aware of their responsibility towards others. In this respect it replicates some of the demands of 'real life' situations. Even if it is not used in the final mark, peer assessment can form a useful exercise for students in viewing the work of others and developing their own work. For example, Tsai *et al* (2001) describe a system where students upload homework to a system, which randomly assigns peers as reviewers. They grade their fellow students' work and comment anonymously. The teacher also grades and comments. The students are notified by the system of their grades and comments, and then modify their work according to these. This is repeated and the work is finally graded by the teacher. Similarly, Macdonald (2001) describes how peer assessment was used to improve students' essay performance.

Another means of involving the students in the assessment process is that of negotiating the criteria of assessment with the educator. Here the students set goals regularly with the educator and discuss how they should be judged against these (eg Boyd and Cowan, 1985). Such an approach encourages student reflection, since they must critically examine their own performance and set themselves suitable goals. It also allows for differences in ability, and gives students a sense of commitment to the learning process. It can be difficult for them, since they are unaccustomed to this way of working and will be unsure what is actually required from them in the course. As with peer assessment, it raises issues about the validity of the assessment and can be stressful for students and educator alike.

Web sites

In Chapter 7 it was suggested that educators needed to integrate the use of the Net into their everyday practice. The same might be said of students, and one way of achieving this is to make the assessment format a Web site. Such a format encourages students in what might be termed 'Web thinking', as they begin to appreciate the issues involved in managing, evaluating and representing information on the Web. The other advantages of such an approach are:

- Students have a greater sense of ownership and personalization than with a standard essay, because they can create Web pages incorporating a number of different design elements.
- It encourages students to use the Web as a resource, incorporating images and links to back up their ideas.
- A non-linear document can be created, with multiple linked pages, which may be more suitable for some subjects.
- Students gain an appreciation of the importance of design and presentation of information.

There are a number of possible disadvantages also, which need to be carefully addressed by the educator:

- Students can focus on the technical or design aspect of the material to the detriment of the actual content.
- There may be a rise in the occurrence of plagiarism (see below).
- Technical problems may detract from student performance.

Much of this will depend on the course and the topic being covered. If the course itself is about Web design, then the disadvantages are merely factors students have to engage with. If the course is in an unrelated subject, then the educator and the students do not want to spend valuable time dealing with technical issues. Some of this can be overcome by the use of templates, which provide a blank set of pages for students to complete. The navigation and structure can then be pre-determined, so students can focus on content. The marking allocation can also be used to reinforce the desired message concerning the importance of content. If the design, technical functionality or code are given a high quota of marks, then students will focus their attentions on producing impressive looking Web sites. If these are allocated relatively few, or no, marks, then the effort will focus on the content.

Portfolios

The use of an end of course portfolio has been a common approach in the arts, but increasingly it is being adopted in other subject areas. Students can be asked to incorporate different examples of activities they have engaged in throughout the course, for example an essay, a course exercise, samples of a conference discussion, and evaluation of other Web sites. These can form the portfolio in its entirety, or students can be requested to comment upon them, for example explaining how an exercise relating to a diagram demonstrates the principles of perspective, or how an exchange in a conference illustrates the issues associated with group learning. Students can also be asked to provide examples of their work that demonstrate evidence of meeting the course objectives, for example a piece of work that illustrates the student has gained an understanding of the binary system. The portfolio is then assessed by how well the examples meet the learning objectives of the course.

As Heywood (2000: 341) points out, 'little is known about the advantages and disadvantages of portfolios in higher education', so it is difficult to make definite claims for them. One of the possible advantages of portfolio based assessment is that it encourages reflection upon the course and the student's performance. Often students do not revisit earlier work in a course and it is easily forgotten. A portfolio approach can be used to encourage students to reflect critically on their own work and the course content as a whole.

Another possible benefit is that a portfolio approach provides an incentive to participate throughout the course, and not simply in topics related to the assessment. This can be used to reward elements that are not easily covered in a conventional content related exam, such as group participation and study skills.

The validation process needs to be carefully implemented in portfolio assessment in order to avoid students passing off others' work as their own.

Plagiarism

This is one of the areas that causes great anxiety among many educators when they discuss online courses. Such concerns, although not completely unfounded, can be exaggerated. If educators are unfamiliar with distance education, it is this aspect rather than the online element that is the major concern, although being online does bring its own set of problems. Distance education establishments originally met the demands of ensuring the validity of assessment by using conventional exams, where a proof of identity was required. As more courses implemented project based assessment, different means of ensuring the identity of the author were developed. As mentioned previously, these can include verification by the student's tutor who has been interacting with the student throughout the year, or a random selection of telephone vivas which act as a deterrent. Online courses can use similar approaches.

The concerns regarding the possibility of cheating in online courses are often based on a misplaced sense of the invulnerability of traditional assessment to any form of plagiarism. In truth, with enough money and effort almost any assessment method can be cheated. Combating plagiarism is much like the battle against computer viruses. There is a tension between making the system accessible and easy to use for the majority of users and preventing the damage caused by those with different intentions. It is the task of educators and universities to place sufficient hurdles in the way that the effort required to cheat successfully actually exceeds that simply to pass the assessment.

What the Net does mean is that there is a vast proliferation of answers and course related material readily available to students. This applies to all courses and not just those online. There are a number of sites that offer essays either free of charge or for a fee. Indeed, the online course is perhaps better suited to detecting this than other courses, since the marker will be familiar with what is available, whereas it might not occur to a marker on a traditional course to check the Web for answers. Even when students have not made such a blatant attempt at cheating, it is still the case that text from other Web sites can be used without being properly attributed. This can occur as a deliberate attempt at plagiarism, or simply because students do not appreciate the boundaries of acceptable behaviour. This is increasingly common where students are encouraged to use the Web in researching and compiling their answers. The educator in this case needs to ensure that students appreciate what is an appropriate use of the Net and what is required of them. Given that students themselves will create Web sites, what this does mean is that reuse of essay titles in different presentations of a course will be problematic.

The use of powerful search engines can detect the more blatant attempts at plagiarism, and there are also a number of specialist software packages or services available to detect plagiarism (eg www.plagiserve.com, CaNexus' Eve and www.plagiarism.org). Perhaps the most effective way of alleviating such concerns is to move away from conventional forms of assessment that are vulnerable to the easy distribution of information. When students did not have much contact with each other and their access to resources was limited, such assessment was reasonably secure, but the ease of communication and access to information renders it no longer so. If some of the approaches outlined in this chapter are adopted, these plagiarism issues are lessened. A focus on the process of interaction and reflection on one's own work is much less easy simply to copy from elsewhere.

Award board issues

For exam or award boards, the use of such assessment, particularly Web sites, raises a number of issues. Plagiarism has already been addressed, but the use of a technology based format raises new questions in the assessment process. Some of these are outlined below.

Compatibility and testing

If students are creating Web sites, or even word processor documents, the question of format compatibility inevitably arises. Unless students have an understanding of HTML standards, they may well include elements that are incompatible with one browser. For any course adopting a Web site assessment format, this raises the issue of to what extent students need to be familiar with HTML, and where the responsibility lies in checking the material. Is it down to the student to test the site in different browsers, or does it lie with the examiner to try alternatives if a problem arises? The use of templates and emphasis on content can overcome this to an extent.

Assignment submission routes

How the assignment is submitted raises both technical and procedural issues for educators and institutions. As I have mentioned in a previous chapter, some institutions adopt a central assignment submission system, which will accept various electronic formats. Such a system can be used to perform a variety of standard functions such as virus checking, storing copies, examining the validity of the format, maintaining deadlines and issuing automatic reminders. Inevitably, though, any centralized system results in a loss of flexibility, at the cost of providing reassurance. For instance, making an automatic copy of every submission prevents students from altering their work after the deadline and then appealing against marks. However, it can also add an element of doubt for students, since they feel that it is the system that is responsible for any problems with their assignment.

Alternatively, students can upload Web sites to their own personal area, and the educator can mark online, or the assignment can be e-mailed directly to the tutor. Provision of a personal Web area offers a number of benefits, since it removes the need for students to locate all of the appropriate files comprising their assignment and send these to the educator or the central system. With a Web site the educator and student are viewing the same material, so responsibility for errors cannot be displaced to a submission system. Unless date restrictions for uploading are implemented it does raise the issue of students continually updating work, since those who are marked later may have had longer to work on their assignment.

A central system can be used to provide students with support and additional functionality. For instance, Chang (2001) describes a system for creating Web based portfolios which helps students with tasks such as compilation, viewing, guidance and discussion, and also provides data on the student learning process.

Any centrally supported system is determined by the assessment demands of educators, but the reverse is also true: the provision of such a system begins to alter the manner in which assessment is performed. Collis, De Boer and Slotman (2001) describe how a Web based assignment system has altered the assessment in many courses, with a move away from large chunks of assessment (such as exams) to smaller components.

Range of software

This is related to the issue of compatibility and provision of a central system. If the software students can use in creating their assignment is limited, some of the unpredictability in the format can be removed. If the software is provided by the course, then a firm line with software can be taken, but if it is the students' own software, then a more open approach may be necessary. With the creation of Web sites it is very difficult to enforce one HTML editor, since it is easy to change the HTML code to specify one tool has been used, even if it has not. By recommending a freely available editor the educator can strongly encourage the use of one piece of software, stipulating that any variation in this is at the student's discretion and runs the risk of producing assignments that cannot be marked.

Some educators prefer to insist on the use of 'raw' HTML in creating Web sites, that is, using a text editor to create a Web document by inserting the appropriate HTML tags. This overcomes some of the problems that arise from using powerful HTML editors, which hide much of their functionality from the user. The Web pages created by such editors can look attractive, and have added functionality, but are often incompatible with certain browsers or server software. They also have a tendency to influence the student in concentrating on design aspects rather than content. However, with increased awareness of using the Web and such tools, it is difficult to insist on raw HTML, and many students feel that this detracts from the benefits the medium offers. Unless HTML coding is taught explicitly in the course, then knowledge of it cannot be assumed.

Graceful degradation

A term often applied to hardware or software is its ability (or more often inability) to 'degrade gracefully'. This means that when something goes wrong, the software can still function in some form: it does not simply cease to operate. Humans are very good at graceful degradation: if a situation is not exactly as anticipated, then a person's behaviour is quickly adjusted to suit the new demands. Computers are less capable of this flexibility. In terms of the Web, graceful degradation is often used to describe Web pages which incorporate more advanced technical or design elements but will degrade to a simpler, yet still functional page if the viewer does not have the right software to interpret these elements. For example, if a Web page relies on Javascript for some of its functionality and the viewer is using an old Web browser that does not interpret Javascript, then a plain text version of the page is displayed.

The use of technical submission formats gives rise to this issue of graceful degradation in assessment, compared with a paper based exam. If there is a problem it often means the assignment is simply unmarkable. For instance, if the student has used a different format, it is unviewable in a browser, or there has been a technical problem in the submission, then the marker simply will not be able to access the work. With paper based scripts one can make an attempt at reading bad handwriting, but the equivalent flexibility is often removed from an electronic assignment.

This may mean that award boards have to make decisions that are less clear cut than was previously the case. An exam has a set of rules, and if the student does not follow them then the decisions are straightforward. Once a technical element is introduced, this adds another element for consideration. Did a problem arise because of a fault with the submission system, or was it down to the student? Was it a problem of compatibility? If so, where does the responsibility lie? Because the electronic assignment might not degrade gracefully, the consequences can be severe: that is, the student would score zero marks. The award board therefore needs to decide upon categories of problem that should permit a resubmission and those that should not. The types of problems that are encountered will soon be recognized and steps taken to address them as much as possible, but it will involve the award board in making decisions and defining procedures that are different in type from those on conventional award boards. These may not fit easily with the existing institutional guidelines, which were designed with the traditional exam as a basic assumption.

Lessons for implementation

1   Rethink assessment methods and procedures

Because many educators have lived with the conventional exam or outcomes based assessment for all of their professional lives, it can assume an aura of inevitability – 'This is the way assessment has to be.' Like almost everything else we take for granted in education, current assessment methods were solutions to specific problems and needs. The conventional exam arose because it suited the demands of a campus education, provided a conclusion to a course and offered some guarantee against cheating in a convenient format. As with much else, online courses create different demands for students and educators, and merely trying to force existing assessment methods to meet these will often result in a poor fit. The distance aspect of some students on online courses is an obvious barrier to conventional exams, but more significantly they do not match the approach of such courses or the learning outcomes. If a constructivist pedagogy has been employed, then it requires flexibility in assessment, since its very philosophy claims that learning is an individual activity, therefore the idea of a model answer is difficult to square with this. Even if a more didactic approach has been used, it is likely that students will have been interacting with a range of media and technology. To sit a conventional exam is somewhat anachronistic compared with the rest of the learning experience. It is not just the conventional exam that is out of place here, but most standard essays similarly fail to match the students' experience of technology or pedagogy of online courses.

If the way that assessment is realized is altered, then the accompanying procedures likewise need to be adapted or overhauled. Again the temptation is to think that the procedures accompanying assessment that deal with issues such as validation, plagiarism, marking, quality control, and so forth are in some way absolute. They too have been devised to meet specific needs, and are usually derived from assumptions about the format of assessment based on the exam and standard projects. It is not that these issues are not important, but rather that institutions need to find new means of addressing them. There needs to be a willingness on the part of the institution to accommodate the needs of online courses and make changes in assessment practice if the educator is not to be distracted by the demands of matching the assessment to the existing procedures.

2   Strike a balance

As with much of the change wrought by online education, any innovation is about striking a balance between competing forces. Here are some of the compromises that need to be struck for types of online assessment:

● The robustness provided by enforcing one specific software package against the individuality and access benefits of allowing free choice.
● An encouragement to participate by allocating marks for group outcomes against rewarding individual contribution.
● The possibilities provided by a Web based format against the technical barrier and issues it creates for students.
● The benefits provided by a central admission system against the flexibility of submitting direct to the educator.
● The need to innovate in assessment format against the need to maintain assessment standards.

Inevitably, the assessment of any course will be a compromise between such factors. This can be achieved while still meeting the learning objectives of the course, if educators and those they need to interact with are aware of the competing demands that they are attempting to satisfy. To this end it is useful to draw up a list of such forces at the outset of a course, and to ensure that the assessment is designed with the learning objectives of the course in mind. Without such an approach there is a danger that the most stubborn of the forces, or the one with the most vociferous proponent, will win out.

Conclusion

The nature of technology mediated interaction with the material, and the underlying philosophy of many online pedagogies, mean that the traditional exam and even outcome based assessment are often no longer suitable. Educators therefore need to develop forms of assessment that match these demands. They need to be supported in this endeavour by adaptability and flexibility in the assessment procedures, regulations and technology implemented by the institution. Issues such as plagiarism, group work and the creation of a technical barrier can be addressed by careful use of assessment methods that strike a balance between the competing forces.

The assessment approach adopted on a course will be strongly influenced by its pedagogy. The technology a course utilizes will also have an impact on the nature of assessment, since it will determine what tools students have available, and what can be expected of them. In the next chapter we will look at this second major influence in an online course after pedagogy, namely technology and media.

Summary

In this chapter we have looked at some of the issues relating to assessment. The following issues have been addressed:

- the role of collaborative work in assessment and issues associated with rewarding group work;
- the decrease in exam based assessment and rise in the use of more project formats for online courses;
- the use of automatic assessment;
- other types of online assessment including use of the Web as a resource, peer assessment, development of student Web sites and the compilation of portfolios;
- plagiarism;
- new concerns for award boards, including compatibility and testing, assignment submission methods, the range of student software and graceful degradation of assignments.

From these, two lessons for implementation were drawn:

- The need to rethink assessment methods and procedures.
- The necessity of striking a suitable balance between competing tensions.

Chapter 9

Technology and media

Introduction

One of the benefits of an online course is the ease with which different types of technology and media can be integrated into the material. Unlike in traditional distance education courses, these do not need to be separated out as distinct elements, such as audio and videotapes, printed units and CD ROMs. The user can access them as required and does not need to break off from a current activity to engage in something else. Even with face to face courses, there is an element of division between components, so experimentation (in the form of laboratory work) is spatially and temporally separated from the theory (in the form of the lecture), which is then separated from discussion in tutorials, and so on. In fairness, there is also a strong element of continuity in face to face courses, as the students will be working within the same group, with the same lecturers and with a strong thematic thread between the theoretical and laboratory based work. The divisions arise partly because of the different requirements of physical space, and the need for scheduling classes in those spaces, which does not hold for a virtual space.

The Net allows students to engage with each element as they need them. For instance while students are reading about a topic they can go to a discussion forum to raise a query, or watch a video clip demonstrating the process. Maintaining a good mix of technology and media can strengthen the appeal of an online course. Bates (1995: 13), referring to traditional distance education courses, suggests that 'decision makers should therefore try to ensure that all four media (print, audio, television, computers) are available for teaching purposes... This will give variety to a course, not only providing an individual learner with different ways of approaching the same material, but accommodating different learning styles.' Web based courses allow these media to be incorporated within one interface. As mentioned in the first chapter, part of the Web's appeal is this generic, comfortable interface.

Each individual media type can usually be better served by a distinct technology designed for that purpose alone. For instance, text in the form of printed units is more portable and easier to read than a Web site. Video in the form of videocassettes or DVD offers better quality than streamed video. What the Internet offers is a means of combining these and allowing students to interact with them in different ways. This is an example of its being a disruptive technology. Although initially weaker than established technologies in certain features, it offers something different, which makes it appealing to a different audience.

In this chapter we will look at some of the main technologies and media relating to online courses and some of the technology influencing the delivery of online courses. Perhaps the most significant technology is that which facilitates communication, be it synchronous or asynchronous. This is not included in this chapter since it has already been covered in an earlier chapter. The media and technologies are addressed here at a general level, rather than reviews of specific products, which will rapidly be out of date.

Text and images

These are not the most revolutionary formats, but ones which form the basis of most online courses. Text occupies the same role in online education as speech does in a campus based course. It represents the primary teaching, exchange, feedback and guidance medium. Text forms the glue that binds together any of the other elements of an online course. In many ways text is better suited to the aims of education than speech. Whereas listening is often a passive activity, reading requires participation and effort. As Umberto Eco (1994: 28) has said, 'text is a lazy machine that expects a lot of collaboration from the reader'. The reader, or in our case the student, therefore has to take an active part in the reading process. Active participation is generally thought to be beneficial in education, so the nature of engaging with text lends itself to education.

Writing for the Web and for students requires some practice and is not the same as writing for paper. First, text on a Web site needs to be chunked to aid reading onscreen. Use of paragraphs, headings and images will help to break up text, and the division of text into separate Web pages will aid the reader. Second, the text itself needs to be as clear and unambiguous as possible. What may seem like a perfectly clear explanation to you can be subject to different interpretations by students. This is why critical readers are important in developing online materials. Third, the text needs to be phrased as a teaching text: that is, it should be directed at students, guiding them through study, with the use of questions to provoke interaction and dialogue with the text itself.

If the course includes a number of articles, then it may be beneficial for students to have these in a format such as Adobe Acrobat's PDF. This provides clear text and aids reading onscreen and printing. The full version of Acrobat (as opposed to the reader, which is free) also includes a number of tools such as the ability to add comments and notes to a document. These can be used to produce shared learning documents.

Although text can be adapted for online suitability, many students find it difficult to read onscreen. It can be more time-consuming and more difficult to extract meaning from onscreen documents. Many students will therefore opt to print out much of the online text. This also addresses the issue of portability, since the printed pages can be read elsewhere. If the course contains a lot of text, then printer-friendly versions (with a simple layout, fewer graphics and formatted for economical paper usage) are advisable. However, much of the urge to print out text derives from prior study habits. This can be overcome by developing study skills that utilize the capabilities of computers and the Internet. For example, students can be encouraged to keep an online journal which contains information and URLs they have found on the Web as well as their own comments. By using hypertext they can create different categories for this material and organize it in different ways, provoking abstraction and deeper analysis of their notes in a way that is difficult to achieve with a paper format. This is part of the value that can be added to an online course over standard print.

The benefits of images are, of course, well known in education. They can be useful in explaining concepts, processes, and also in providing context. In online courses they are also useful in breaking up intimidating chunks of text and enlivening material. Students will vary in their learning styles and preferences. Some will have a more visual style of learning, and for these students it is useful to include diagrams that explain concepts already covered in the text. Much of this will depend on the type of course being offered. If it is a large-scale course with little educator support, then material that explains concepts in different ways is advisable. If the course is based around discussion and interaction with the educator, then the need for such a variety of material in the Web site is lessened. We will look at this influence of the type of course in more detail in the next chapter.

When using images, there are two issues to be borne in mind regarding the student experience. The first is download times. If students are accessing via modems, then pages with lots of images can be frustrating to download. The images themselves need to be formatted for Web delivery (usually in JPEG format) and be of a suitably low file size, whilst maintaining the image quality. This will be less of an issue as high bandwidth access, broadband, becomes increasingly common. The second issue is accessibility. For blind or partially sighted students, a Web site that relies heavily on images is disadvantaging. If every page contains a great many images, it is also irritating for the student who is using screen reader software if there is no description of the image. Careful use of the Alt tag in HTML, which describes the image, and text versions of Web sites, can overcome these problems to an extent.

Video and audio

The use of video divides opinion among online educators. For some, video is the main feature of an online course, while others view it as an additional element, which has some disadvantages. Video has many educational benefits that can enhance an online course if it is implemented correctly. These include:

- Adding variety to the material and enlivening topics.
- Demonstrating situations and environments that are difficult to do so otherwise, such as life in other countries, industrial processes.
- Providing context and concrete examples, thereby making material more meaningful for students, such as clips of a person featured in the material, or examples of engineering principles.
- Guiding students through physical tasks, such as preparing food or developing a painting technique.
- Allowing student control, so it can be viewed at their own pace and reviewed.
- As with images, it appeals to the learning style of some students.

It has a number of disadvantages, however, which limit its use in online courses:

- Quality can be poor over standard telephone connections. Compression techniques and the use of video that is not very image intensive, for example a talking head against a blank background, can alleviate this. As bandwidth increases this will be less of an issue.
- Download times can be excessive. If students are accessing the video via standard modems, then even small clips can take a long time to download. The use of streaming video servers lessens this to a degree, since the video can be playing while the remainder is still downloading. These still require the user to download a sufficient proportion of the video to a buffer to ensure a smooth presentation. Again this will be less of an issue if high-bandwidth access is commonplace.
- It is difficult to maintain attention with long video clips, particularly if they are of a small resolution and poor in quality.
- They are essentially passive, so the student does not interact with them.
- Not all subjects are suited to video. Topics that have a high visual impact are best served by video.
- They can disadvantage blind or deaf students, unless transcripts of the audio are provided.
- There may be software or hardware problems. With the robustness of standard plug-in software such as QuickTime from Apple, and RealPlayer this is less of an issue, but some students may encounter difficulties.

The cost of video can be seen as both an advantage and disadvantage. It is relatively inexpensive to buy a Web-cam or digital video camera, and the software required to produce video clips is also not expensive. So producing and delivering video can be done by an individual, without the need for much of the special equipment that was necessary in producing analogue audio/visual material. However, this is largely because the quality of online video is poor, so there is little to be gained from expensive video production. As bandwidth restrictions become less limiting, then the quality of online video will increase. There will be a subsequent rise in the cost of producing effective video, since good-quality educational video benefits enormously from professional production methods, storyboarding, editing, and so on.

I have argued earlier that the use of video to deliver lectures via the Net is an ineffective teaching approach for online courses. This is not to say that video is not useful in a course, or that a video lecture cannot be used very effectively. Video should just not be the sum of a course. In conjunction with other media and within an appropriate teaching strategy, video can add a lot to a course. If it is used heavily, then the key to its success is to require students to do something with it. For example, a video lecture can be the basis for a discussion, or students can be asked to analyse the contents of a clip with reference to a theory they have learnt. Interactive video that incorporates other multi-media elements such as animation and allows students to add comments and notes is now more of a reality with tools such as Flash. This is another means of making video a resource with which students have to interact.

Much of the early enthusiasm for online education, particularly from the commercial sector, focused on the idea of video lectures. The idea of an infinite lecture hall has enormous financial appeal, but in reality it underestimates the role of the educator. In an investigation comparing video delivery with face to face lecturing, Smith and Ransbottom (2000) found that students in the face to face lecturer group demonstrated a deeper understanding of the material. They conclude that while video is good at many things, 'it can't provide guidance, however. It can't manage a student's time or provide motivation and inspiration. It can't adjust its teaching style based on body language or blank stare.' There are online equivalents of a blank stare, such as the student who does not contribute, or does not log in to the system even, and it is this inability to interact with the students and adapt that ultimately makes video a useful but not essential tool.

Audio is more robust over the Net and can achieve reasonably good quality. As with video, it is difficult for a student to listen to long clips of audio and maintain interest and concentration. They are obviously useful in subjects with a high auditory element such as language, poetry and music. Audio can also be used to provide a sense of online presence or of atmosphere in a simulation. By combining it with still photographs, a low-bandwidth version of a presentation can be created. It is also useful for guiding students through tasks they can perform at the computer: for example, training in software packages – since the student can listen while performing the task.

Computer assisted learning (CAL)

CAL, or computer based training (CBT), gained popularity with the growth in use of personal computers in the 1980s. As with many such terms, it is difficult to find a definition that is widely agreed upon. It can include multi-media applications, animations, simulations, microworlds, programming languages, and even any application of computers in education. For the purpose of this discussion, let us take it to mean any software program that is designed to teach a specific topic through user interaction. As with much of educational technology, there was some hyperbole surrounding CAL in its early days. Many thought it would mean the computer replacing the teacher. Many useful packages were developed, but CAL did not have the impact many predicted. The Internet has seen a revival of interest from many quarters in CAL.

The advantages of CAL are that:

- it enlivens material by making the student interact with it;
- its interactivity promotes active learning;
- it demonstrates some ideas that are difficult to explain in text: for example, processes and interactions;
- it promotes exploratory learning by providing simulations;
- it is self-paced and controlled by the student;
- it allows students to explore impossible, dangerous or expensive scenarios such as alternative worlds, radiation equipment and circuit boards.

The use of Net-delivered CAL seems better suited to the needs of education than video in many respects. CAL can suit any pedagogical approach: for instance, it can be used in straightforward instruction by having a set of fixed sequence animations or tests. In the form of simulation it is well suited to subjects with a practical element. Ronen and Eliahu (2000) suggest that simulation provides a means to bridge the gap between the theory students learn and what happens in reality. CAL can also be incorporated into constructivist approaches through the use of open-ended microworlds or simulations, which allow students to explore a particular topic and create a personalized experience. For example, Edelson, Pea and Gomez (1996: 157) describe a system called CoVis (for collaborative visualization) that encourages high school students to use scientific visualization tools to pose their own research questions, investigate these through manipulation of data, and generate images to demonstrate them. These images then form the basis for debate. Such an approach can be regarded as a form of legitimate peripheral participation, since it uses a version of the tools used by academics in the field. They provide the example of the 'climate visualizer to conduct investigations into topics of their own choosing that include the effect of coastlines on local temperatures, the impact of volcanoes on weather, and what the climate will be like in California in 50 million years'.

CAL is not without its drawbacks, however:

- It can be expensive to produce. Because CAL is aimed at teaching a specific topic, idea or concept, there is often nothing available 'off the shelf'. This means educators have to produce the CAL they need. It is time-consuming to develop CAL that will be engaging for students, as it requires programming, design, storyboarding, and so on.
- It requires some specialist knowledge and skills to produce. There are a number of tools available that simplify the task of producing CAL, but even so they require some time and effort to master and will not be usable by all educators. In addition, a CAL package may require specialist skills, such as design or interactivity expertise.
- Students can engage with it at a superficial level: that is, manipulating the CAL variables becomes the focus of activity without understanding why the changes occur.
- There is not much evidence that CAL actually improves learning in terms of retention of knowledge or demonstrating a deeper understanding of the material.

Given the potential cost of developing CAL packages, their use needs to be carefully planned. For some topics, particularly in the training market, they can be very cost-effective since they can provide sufficient guidance and inter-activity that a human is not required to offer support. For most higher education courses this is unlikely to be the case, so they need to provide some benefits for the students and also reduce some of the educator's teaching burden. However, one of the benefits of Net based courses is that they do offer a convenient means of combining different media and technologies. In this respect the addition of CAL is one way in which online courses can add rich-ness and avoid the accusation of merely being a textbook on the Web. The use of CAL packages will vary in courses, depending on the topic, the market audience and the pedagogy used. We will look at this further in the following chapter.

Virtual worlds

An early innovation on the Net was the use of multi-user virtual worlds, where each user adopted a different identity. These were initially text based and focused on fantasy role-playing games, hence they were termed MUDs (multi-user dungeons). These have broadened out somewhat and have become visually based, and are now termed MUSEs (multi-user simulation environments). These have attracted some interest in education, since they allow constructivist, open-ended environments. Dede (1996) states that 'through underlying software models such as distributed simulation, a learner can be immersed in a synthetic, constructivist environment. The student acts and collaborates not as himself or herself, but behind the mask of an "avatar": a surrogate persona in the virtual world.' This networked, multi-user approach has become increasingly popular with computer games.

Although they are intriguing and enjoyable, my feeling is that their educational use can be limited, although in certain subject areas their use in role-playing can be beneficial. They can also be used to develop team-building skills, to experience different interactions as a result of gender or personality alterations, to explore the development of communities and social constraints, or to work collaboratively within certain scenarios. In order for this to be successful, the altered personality of a person in the MUSE can be detrimental – since students need to feel a responsibility towards each other. They are also expensive to create from scratch if realistic visuals are required. They appeal to certain users, for example those who enjoy role-playing games, but equally many people find them rather offputting.

Virtual worlds do not have to be multi-user; they can be used by an individual. Many existing games fall into this category and some of these can be used in education: for example, Electronic Arts' SimCity game, where students devise cities, can be a useful teaching device about the contrasting pressures in any modern conurbation. Students can each create their own cities, perhaps with different specifications, and then exchange and discuss these. For example, Adams (1998) used it to teach urban geography concepts and reported good motivation and evidence of 'attitudinal learning' regarding the role of urban planners.

As with CAL, the danger of virtual worlds is that they have a strong game play element. This is useful in providing motivation, stimulation and interest, but it can also be detrimental in that the student focus is on how to 'play the game' rather than the educational content. Placing such elements within a strong pedagogic framework that emphasizes discussion and analysis is necessary if this is to be avoided. They are also very time-consuming for students to use, so the learning outcomes need to be a significant element of the course if this time is to be justified.

Intelligent agents

The advent of artificial intelligence in the 1980s and early 1990s led to its application as an educational technology. This was seen particularly with the development of intelligent tutoring systems (ITS). The idea behind these was that, as with expert systems developed in commercial, medical and industrial spheres, the rules of a human expert could be encapsulated in a computer system. Intelligent systems could be developed that could answer queries, guide students through material, identify and remedy student difficulties and so on. They were better suited to formal domains such as maths and geometry where the rules and skills required are clearly defined, rather than domains that require reading and interpretation, such as literature studies, social sciences and psychology. As with CAL, much of the initial promise surrounding such systems failed to materialize. This was partly a result of the enormous complexity required to represent the domain, identify the possible problems students have, develop a student model of under-standing, and so on. Therefore they tended to be either large university research projects or much smaller in scope and dealing with very limited tasks. Some were developed into useful teaching aids, if not quite the human replacement once envisaged.

In the late 1990s there was a growth in interest in artificial intelligence research in intelligent, autonomous agents. These agents have beliefs, values, behaviours and the ability to learn and make decisions. Much of the research concentrated on the interactions between multiple agents, which often exhibited unexpected and revealing outcomes. The use of such agents on the Internet has also been of interest. Such agents can 'roam' the Internet on behalf of users searching for infor-mation, bidding for items in online auctions and so on.

The application of such agents to education can be viewed as a revival of interest in intelligent tutoring systems. For example, Stamatis *et al* (1999) describe a multi-agent system to help educators and institutions in such tasks as admissions of students and provision of technical support. Albert and Thomas (2000) describe an agent on a management course that aids students in creating an intellectual capital report. Not all of the tutors on the course were experts in this process, so an 'automated tutor' to help students is a way of achieving a larger scale on the course. The agent in question helps students complete the report by directing them through a set of resources.

What separates 'an agent' from merely a set of automated guidelines, such as one might find in a software 'wizard', is supposedly the autonomy and decision making capabilities of the agent. This is not always evident in the educational applications of the term. However, for guidance on specific tasks agents are likely to become increasingly popular, since many of the problems students encounter are well known. Use of agents to solve these means the students can get the help when they need it, and liberates the educator to concentrate on developing higher skills. The drawbacks of intelligent agents are:

● They are developed on a bespoke basis.
● They require programming skills to develop.
● They are very time-consuming to develop since, as with ITSs, they require a full representation of a domain.
● They can be frustrating for students if they do not answer their queries.
● They can remove the educator from some of the necessary dialogue with students.
● They are not as flexible or adaptable as a human educator.
● They may miss, or misinterpret important information from the student.

Data mining

In commercial sites such as Amazon, data mining is used to provide recommendations, so that the purchaser of a certain product receives suggestions as to other products that they may like, based on the data of previous buyers. In education it could be used to provide helpful information about student behaviour. For example, students who get certain questions wrong in an online quiz might tend to go on to fail the course, and those who exhibit certain behaviours such as short log-in times and random page selection often drop out of the course early. Such information could be used to prompt the educator to offer special advice or remedial sessions in order to catch the problem early.

The analysis of user data can also be used by organizations to ensure appropriate training is provided. For instance, Treanor and Irwin (2001) incorporated data from other corporate systems, such as human resources databases, to track an employee's training, to suggest possible courses based on their job area and provide relevant information. Data mining could be combined with intelligent agents, so that certain behaviour patterns might automatically launch a tutoring agent who can offer alternative explanations and material to such students.

Data mining can be used for beneficial purposes, but one should be wary about its use. If students feel they are being monitored continuously, then not only might this be very intrusive, but they might spend time developing what they think is the appropriate behaviour to 'fool' the data collection program. For example, opening each page for a long period does not necessarily mean the student is studying or understanding the content, but it might be the type of indicator which is incorporated in data mining. Similarly, being logged in to the system and sending messages does not mean a student is engaged in academic debate. Data mining, although interesting and potentially useful, is typical of the sort of technology to which some people can attach too much emphasis and optimism.

XML

XML stands for Extensible Markup Language. It is a more flexible and adaptable method of producing Web documents than the current HTML (Hypertext Markup Language). It is a subset of the larger, more complex SGML (Standard Generalized Markup Language), the international standard for defining electronic documents. What XML does is describe data. This means you can define your own styles for a document. This is different from the normal HTML used in most Web documents. HTML has defined styles, so, for example, Heading 1 style always appears the same. With XML you can define how Heading 1 should look. So crucially it is extendable and flexible and not fixed, like HTML.

This allows specialist groups to define their own markup applications, so, for example, musicians might agree formats for music specification, chemists can interchange formulae via agreed markup styles and so on. This is currently difficult with HTML.

For the Web developer it also separates the design of a Web page and the content, whereas HTML embeds these within the same document. This separation makes maintaining a large Web site much easier. For instance, if you wish to change the appearance of your Web site you merely change the defined style sheet once and this will change every page, rather than your needing to alter each page manually. It also facilitates the type of document reusability mentioned in Chapter 7. If you store content in a plain XML format – that is, without any styling – it can be used by different institutions, which can pass it through their own style formatting. Thus the same content can be used in a course at Oxford University and Hong Kong University, say, but it will appear with the corresponding styles and languages of each provider. It can also be used to provide different representations of the content within one course: for example, students can select a presentation style which suits their learning preference, so one student may see the content in a more visual format, another as plain text, and so on.

XML is essentially a meta-language: that is, it is a language about language. As such it describes the style and content each document contains in metadata. These can add great functionality to the Web. Instead of searching the Web for documents that contain certain words, as most search engines do, XML documents declare what type of information they contain. For education this means the Web becomes a more usable resource. This feature also encourages the reusability of content, since the metadata can store information about the content, facilitating effective searching and retrieval.

Lastly, because XML is an agreed standard and is non-proprietary, it is easier to pass information between formats. This removes some of the political and commercial concerns raised when one company owns a format. It also enables sharing between applications, not just the Web. So you may have documents stored centrally in XML which can be delivered as Web pages, on paper, in PDF, and so on.

HTML is easier to learn and use initially, particularly with the number of editors available. For larger sites, and if the material you are developing is going to be reused in any way, then using XML will be more beneficial in the long term. It seems to be the way the Web will develop over the next few years.

Web based course delivery systems

There are a number of systems that allow educators to create and deliver courses and provide a range of functionality. Common examples are WebCT, Blackboard, WBT System's TopClass and Lotus Learning Space. These systems provide templates for creating courses, and remove much of the technical difficulties involved. Typical features of such systems can include:

● communication tools, such as text conferences, e-mail, synchronous voice chat and video conferencing;

- easy-to-use templates for creating pages without any need for HTML expertise;
- a range of styles, images and resources to use;
- easy implementation of multi-media into pages;
- multi-user tools such as whiteboards and shared documents;
- tools for creating online quizzes and assessment;
- Web space and notes areas for students;
- annotation capability;
- tracking systems so student progress can be monitored;
- guidance and tools for creating effective online courses;
- managing student information;
- security and protection;
- technical support.

This removes much of the hassle from creating an online course, so the educator can concentrate on content and pedagogy. Some systems can be purchased to run on university servers, and other suppliers will host the course on their server, charging a fee for each student. Many of the course delivery systems can be linked with existing university systems, for example those responsible for handling student records.

The experience of the many educators who have adopted such systems is often favourable. For example, Alexander reports her experience in implementing TopClass across the university: 'The use of TopClass has grown exponentially and has been successful in improving access to learning activities, improving learning outcomes for students, and improving student attitudes to learning' (Alexander, 1999: 292).

For many institutions and educators, the use of such systems provides a valuable method of realizing online courses that look professional and incorporate a reasonable range of media in a relatively short timescale. There is inevitably something of a trade-off in terms of flexibility, as there is with any 'off the peg' solution, but there is some flexibility and customization potential built into most systems. However, the systems are often designed around a 'classroom' metaphor, which is not always appropriate, and does not always scale effectively. Although such solutions are promoted partly on their flexibility and adaptability, they inevitably suggest certain approaches. For instance, if the system is based around a classroom metaphor, then this may suggest a more didactic approach than a constructivist one. The danger here is that by simply using these packages, educators do not move beyond the standard models they provide. Other institutions have chosen to develop their own systems by integrating different software packages: for instance, one for Web site management, and another for e-mail and communication. Although this may enable greater flexibility, it raises the issue of communication between such systems and initial investment in developing such solutions.

Such systems are not adept at handling large quantities of resources. For such a system, for example a global collection of educational resources, content management systems are better suited, usually storing the resources in XML format.

Lessons for implementation

1 Use a variety of technologies

This will be influenced by the pedagogy you have adopted, and we will look at the relation between pedagogy and technology in the next chapter. As we have seen, the Net is not as good at delivering each media type as technology designed solely for that purpose. It is partly through the smooth integration of these media types that online courses add richness compared with traditional distance education or face to face courses. The other major benefit the online course offers is communication.

Different media will suit different students and learning styles, therefore a mix of media will broaden the appeal of a course and increase its effectiveness.

2 Make the technology cost-effective

Although a mix of media is beneficial, there is a caveat to this, which is that of cost-effectiveness. If a course contains the same information in a variety of formats, its production costs are significantly increased for what is essentially the same material. In addition, students may find it difficult to choose between media types and use all of them, making the workload excessive.

Another aspect of cost-effectiveness is how much the technology relates to the overall learning outcomes of the course and what proportion of the course it constitutes. This is particularly true of any bespoke development, such as CAL or intelligent agents. If these are only a marginal part of the course, then the time and cost in development might not be worthwhile, and similarly the time students spend in engaging with the software might not be reflected in course outcomes.

Before you engage in the development of specialist software it is worth considering the benefit it brings to the course, any potential saving in educator or student time, how it relates to assessment, and what other uses it may have. If it can be adapted for use elsewhere, or if it forms part of the educator's staff development (for instance learning a programming language), then some of the developmental costs can be ignored.

3 Consider the long term with delivery platforms

There is a balance to be struck here. Educators and institutions will gain invaluable experience in actually delivering online courses, so any delay in doing so should be minimized. However, rushing into online delivery can create a legacy of material that is difficult to update or adapt. It can also lead to a diversity of approaches, as each educator adopts a different technology. There is much to be said for a unified approach across an institution, but if this is not forthcoming, individual pilot studies can be useful in gaining experience and providing momentum. For many educators and institutions the best option will be to use one of the existing course delivery systems. These will provide most of the functionality, support and technology necessary without the necessity of the educator becoming an expert in all of these issues. As institutions develop a broader online offering they may decide to develop their own delivery platforms.

The integration of content into future courses and the updating of material are also major considerations. The use of technology that separates content from design, such as XML or HTML style sheets, will significantly aid this.

Conclusion

Technology plays a significant part in an online course. The availability of certain technology can influence the pedagogy a course adopts. The technological environment replaces the physical one for online students, and it represents the space in which students will be learning. Online courses are influenced not only by the media and teaching technologies apparent to students, but also by the choice of implementation platform. Course delivery systems and XML represent some of the significant technologies in this area.

A number of technologies that have not been included here may well be significant in an online course. Some have been subsumed under some of the categories here, or covered in previous chapters: for instance, communication and assessment related technologies. Inevitably in such limited space there will be some omissions which some educators will regard as glaring, but the technologies and media outlined above should give an indication of the possibilities and pitfalls in integrating any technology into an online course.

As with many issues in online education, there is a balance between the time taken to produce and implement such technologies and the benefits they provide for students. The pedagogy a course adopts can have some influence on the rationale for implementing technology. It is this influence of technology on pedagogy and vice versa that we will look at in the next chapter.

Summary

In this chapter we have looked at the types of media that can be incorporated into an online course and some of the associated advantages and disadvantages of each. The technologies and media addressed were:

- text and images;
- audio and video;

- CAL;
- virtual worlds;
- intelligent agents;
- data mining;
- course delivery systems;
- XML.

These technologies have raised three lessons for implementation:

- Use a variety of technologies where possible.
- Make the technology cost effective.
- Consider long-term issues with delivery platforms.

Chapter 10

A framework for classifying online courses

Introduction

In previous chapters we have looked at pedagogy and technology as they relate to online courses. Some educators suggest that pedagogy should always be the driving factor in course design. This view has some merits, in that it is easy to be seduced by technology without necessarily considering its usefulness in a course. As Bates (1995: 12) comments, 'Good teaching may overcome a bad choice in the use of technology, but technology will never save bad teaching; usually it makes it worse.'

However, the pedagogy in turn will be influenced by the technology available and what it makes feasible. For instance, if students can add comments to a Web page, without altering the page, then group annotation of an article becomes a viable activity. The technology not only allows the approach to be realized, but it suggests it, by making a functionality available which the educator might not have previously considered.

Technology and pedagogy are thus intertwined in any online course. In creating such a course much of the initial effort is expended in determining these two factors. What pedagogy will the course adopt and what technology can be used to support this? This is an iterative process: the fine details of the pedagogy will be shaped by the decisions made about technology and vice versa, as educators seek out technological solutions to pedagogic demands and envisage new pedagogical approaches as technology offers new functionality.

In this chapter a framework for classifying online courses is described, which incorporates these twin pillars. The focus is on courses that are predominantly or solely delivered online, rather than those that use the Net as a support for face to face teaching. Such a framework provides a useful means of addressing the demands of the broad range of online courses. It also illustrates how there can be such a diversity of views as to the form online education does, or should, take. It is these views that are at the heart of the different opinions regarding the benefits or dangers of online education.

A framework for classifying online courses

The framework has two axes along which online courses can be classified, giving four broad categories. These two axes represent the influence of technology and pedagogy on the course. The y-axis has a continuum ranging from low technology to high technology. This indicates the degree of technological sophistication embedded within the course. This can be determined by a number of technical elements, some examples of which include:

- range of media, including audio, video and animations;
- use of interactive elements such as quizzes, games and user controlled animations;
- degree of personalization offered, so students can create their own individual environment;
- use of sophisticated back-end systems to allow for functions such as tracking students, annotation of pages and personal logs;
- Web site design, navigation and interactivity;
- communication environments which encourage and facilitate dialogue.

The extent to which such elements are incorporated in an online course will determine its technological richness.

The x-axis represents the second major element in any online course design, namely pedagogy. Here the continuum is less straightforward, since it is not a simple gradation. The poles for this axis can be termed 'didactic' and 'constructivist'. This represents the shift from a traditional, instructional based teaching approach, to a more constructivist, student centred one. There is no judgement implied by placing them on an axis, but the implication is that courses can implement one of these two differing approaches in extreme, or combine a mix of the two elements. 'Didactic' is a term that is used in a variety of contexts and with differing meanings. It can be used synonymously with teaching, but is often meant to portray a teacher directed style. For this framework a didactic approach is one which incorporates the following teaching styles:

- an emphasis on content;
- assessment to test the understanding and retention of content;
- an emphasis on correct answers, or absolute truths to be conveyed;
- instructional techniques such as lectures and textual explanation;

- behaviourist learning approaches such as explain and test;
- the educator in the role of expert.

Constructivism has been covered in Chapter 5. Courses towards the constructivist end of the classification will exhibit some of the following characteristics:

- an emphasis on student interaction;
- assessment that focuses on process and student interpretation;
- an emphasis on students' own experiences and their understanding of concepts;
- use of techniques such as dialogue and collaborative working;
- learning as a social activity;
- the educator in the role of facilitator and possibly mentor.

Many courses that claim to have a constructivist approach will often incorporate elements from the first list, and to a lesser extent (but increasingly constructivist influences are being picked up on) the reverse is true, so the absolute extremes are likely to be rare.

This framework is outlined in Figure 10.1. It gives us four broad categories in which to categorize online courses, which can now be examined in more detail.

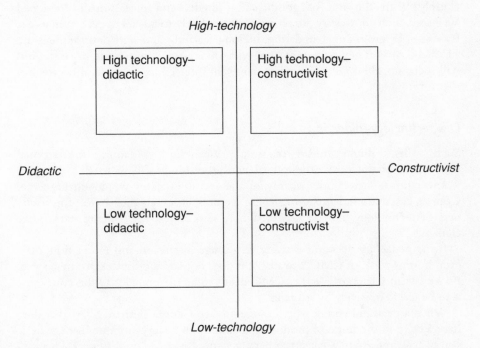

Figure 10.1 *The pedagogy–technology framework for classifying online courses*

Categorizing online courses

If we look at each of the categories in turn, some of the issues associated with online delivery can be addressed.

High technology–didactic

Courses that can be deemed high technology and didactic in approach represent much of the offering in the Web based training (WBT) area. Such courses usually have a good range of media, are very professional in their design and incorporate a high degree of functionality and interactivity in their Web sites. The pedagogy is usually based around instruction, since these courses are often aimed at individuals who want to sign up at any time and gain some knowledge about a specific area within a reasonably short timespan. Independent study without the need for interaction with others, and clear specification in terms of content, therefore suit this type of student.

Such courses may or may not be supported by a tutor, and the assessment may be in the form of an automatic quiz or exam. It is this type of course that many of those who fear that educators will be replaced by technology have in mind. It can be offered to a large number of students, requires little educator input beyond the initial production, and can therefore be offered relatively cheaply. With the use of good-quality media and professionally designed Web sites, such courses are attractive. They are likely to appeal to certain markets: for example, professional updating, lifelong learning and staff development are all likely areas. They represent the type of course commercial organizations will focus on, although universities may well offer courses that fit this category also.

Low technology–didactic

Such courses might consist of simple Web sites, containing instructional text. Many of the early attempts of educators might fall in to this category. Those courses that consist mainly of the lecturer's notes would qualify here. Courses based around streaming video lectures, although they have some richness of technology, can be classified here also, unless they incorporate other elements.

If the pedagogy does not actively encourage discussion and interaction, then even if some form of CMC is available it does not add a great deal to the course. As we saw in Chapters 5 and 6, CMC needs to be integrated into the course for it to be used effectively by students.

When a beautiful young woman suggested to George Bernard Shaw that they have a baby, in the hope of producing a child with beauty and intelligence, he is said to have retorted, 'What if the baby gets my body and your brains?' This category of course seems to represent this poor mix of the two possibilities: it gains neither the technological richness nor the interactivity the Net offers, but instead the lack of human contact and inflexibility which are always a possibility with a distance education course. With such courses the question is raised as to what benefit they gain from being online. The pedagogy essentially replicates that of face to face teaching, but without many of the benefits that situation offers. By not adding technological richness or integrating communication into the course, these courses do not take advantage of the primary benefits offered by the Net.

This category represents what many of the detractors of the Net in education see as the norm. The motivation behind such courses is mainly to benefit institutions, in that they allow increased reach with relatively little investment in resources, in terms of both technology and people. Since the educator is not actively involved in interaction with the students, a high student to educator ratio can be achieved.

Such courses are increasingly rare, however. When the Web was relatively new and people were becoming accustomed to it, they were more frequent and in many ways more acceptable. Most educators soon realize that they do not offer a very rewarding experience for students, and with later iterations of the course begin to move along one or both of the axes. Similarly, most students have a greater familiarity with the Net and find such courses unattractive and unrewarding.

Low technology–constructivist

Such courses use relatively simple technology: for example, they may focus on a simple Web site containing text and images and an associated CMC technology. They utilize some constructivist elements, however, so much of the learning takes place through communication, dialogue and interaction. This appreciates and takes advantage of one of the key features of the Net, that it facilitates two-way communication.

Many small-scale university courses might fall in to this category. This is particularly likely in topics that are not very technologically oriented but involve a good deal of debate. Examples might be online courses in theology, history, philosophy, and so forth.

By adopting a constructivist approach they can promote collaborative learning and discussion. They do not necessarily require a rich mix of technology, since the subject does not readily lend itself to this, and the students are not particularly interested in, or attracted by, it. If the Net is utilized as a resource, the amount of material the actual course Web site itself needs to contain can be minimized also. What such courses do require is a carefully structured framework within which interaction occurs, and a commitment from the educator to be actively engaged throughout the course. The assessment for such a course needs to be suited to this approach so as to encourage and reward participation.

Technology rich–constructivist

One interpretation of the suggested framework is that this category is the desired goal for all online courses. This is not the case, since this implies a value judgement. I am not suggesting that constructivism is superior to a didactic approach, but rather that courses need to make appropriate use of the Net, and be suitable for their target audience. Adopting a constructivist approach, or providing a rich technological environment, is one way of achieving this.

It is possible to do both, and indeed one can usefully support the other. A high technology environment might include functions that aid the educator, such as the ability to create different communication spaces with different features, or tools for promoting group work which include synchronous and asynchronous communication tools, shared whiteboards, document annotating devices, and so on. The course content might also include media such as virtual environments that allow students to explore ideas and concepts, or engage in experimentation.

Such courses may be better suited to some domains than others. For example, design, engineering, and scientific subjects may benefit from having such online tools in which students can engage in a form of legitimate peripheral participation, often working in teams.

Costs associated with online courses

Using the above framework we can look at the issue of cost and how it relates to online courses. There are two components to the cost of a course: those costs arising in the production of the course, and those associated with its delivery or presentation.

The degree of technology richness will largely influence the production costs of a course. Producing a range of media and developing rich functionality and interactivity require input from a number of people in the design, production and testing phases. It could be argued that a didactic approach also requires a high production phase, since it generally carries more content than a constructivist one. However, a properly designed constructivist course will devote an equal amount of time in developing meaningful activities for the students and the appropriate guidance. This might not always be the case, but it is more difficult to state with confidence that any one pedagogy will result in an increased production load, whereas the level of technology richness will almost certainly have an effect.

The pedagogy does relate more directly to presentation costs, however. Constructivist approaches require a great deal of educator involvement throughout the duration of the course if they are to be successful. The educator needs continually to support, guide, encourage and participate with students as they take on a role of participant in the learning process.

The relative costs of production and presentation associated with the four categories of online courses are summarized in Table 10.1.

Table 10.1 *Costs associated with different online courses*

	Production	Presentation
High technology–didactic	High	Low
Low technology–didactic	Low	Low
Low technology–constructivist	Low	High
High technology–constructivist	High	Medium

High technology–didactic

For many commercial companies offering courses that might be classified as high technology–didactic, the initial production costs are higher than with some of the other approaches (although compared with the costs associated with staff time, travel, room rental, and so on, they may still be much lower than those associated with running face to face courses). They will have a team of technical staff and a variety of tools available and make good use of templates to reduce these costs, but they are still considerable. Much of the content has to be produced from scratch, and such material constitutes a large part of the course. Once the course is produced, however, its presentation costs are relatively low. This will depend largely on the degree of tutor support. Some courses might be entirely without tutor support, using automatic assessment for the end of course test and intelligent agents and data mining to provide support. In such cases the course is free to reproduce, so there is little or no cost associated with each additional student. If the course has some form of assessment marked by a person, or is supported via e-mail, then there is an associated cost with each additional student, but it is less than that of a fully educator centred approach found in face to face education. This may be a result of some costs being hidden or pushed on to other parties: for example, part-time educators working from home use their own equipment, office space, and so on. If the institution were required to contribute towards these costs, then there might be less of a saving.

Therefore, once such a course is created, the emphasis is on getting as many students as possible, so such courses are likely to be offered to the general public. They become profitable once they recoup their initial production costs, so they are confined to topics where such a return is likely. They operate on a large scale, although usually they are offered for take-up at any time, so the load is spread. It is not the case that they rely on a single large cohort of students.

Low technology–didactic

The course that is both low technology and didactic represents the cheapest model for the organization, since it requires little effort in terms of production and presentation. Unless there is a specific market need that is not met elsewhere, such courses are unlikely to succeed in the commercial world since they do not have enough appeal compared with similar offerings from competitors with greater technological richness. One way in which such courses might succeed is by replacing technological richness with 'star quality'. So, for example, streaming lectures of internationally renowned experts might well be attractive for many students.

The drive behind such courses is often one of maximizing resources, so they too are likely to operate on a large scale, although this will often be in the form of a single cohort of students. It is likely that universities and colleges will be the organizations to offer such courses, particularly for large foundation courses that form part of several degree programmes.

Low technology–constructivist

The low technology–constructivist course is likely to be relatively cheap in terms of production, but it will require a great deal of educator input throughout the course, so will be expensive in terms of presentation. For some of the reasons covered in the chapters on communication and new working methods, online courses can create a significant workload for educators. This is particularly the case with a constructivist model, and when there is relatively little technology for students to interact with, the interactions they achieve with fellow students and the educator are the course. Of all the categories, this one probably represents the greatest workload for educators over time. This is significant since it may often appear to be an easy option to implement and one that is pedagogically sound. While this is true, it is likely to command a great deal of the educator's time.

Such courses are more likely to operate on a relatively small scale, usually with one educator and a group of students. They will almost exclusively be offered by universities and colleges, since they do not represent the type of market or approach commercial companies will favour.

High technology–constructivist

The last category, that of high technology–constructivist, seems to offer the worst of both worlds for organizations, in that it is costly to produce and requires a good deal of effort in presentation. There may be some payoff, however, in terms of reducing the presentation load through technology. For this reason the presentation cost is adjudged 'medium' in Table 10.1. Interaction time with the educator can be offset against the time students spend learning through the use of rich tools. Similarly, if the educator is provided with useful tools to help the students in their interaction, the educator can be less involved in facilitating the actual process of collaboration. A similar reduction in production costs by utilizing a constructivist approach to remove the need for some content is less likely. Creating tools that facilitate a constructivist approach is liable to be time-consuming, since they need to be flexible and allow for independent exploration. They are therefore more demanding to create than straightforward animations or video clips. However, once created they can be reused, so a benefit may be found over time.

The high production costs involved in such courses means they will have to recoup these costs in some way: being priced highly; offered on a large scale; or having a long projected life. The constructivist approach means that they will be intensive in presentation, so will probably require more than one educator to support them if they are offered on a large scale. A part-time tutor model, similar to that used by the Open University, will probably be found with such courses. It is universities or commercial organizations that offer distance education on a large scale and have the resources to put into production that will offer such courses. However, such courses represent a shift in the traditional financial model of distance education, which has operated on a Fordist model of industrial scale. Traditionally, course production has been high, but presentation costs have been relatively low. The move to the integration of communication technologies, and particularly a constructivist approach, results in a loss of the economies of scale that operated previously. Bates sums it up thus:

> Since production is the main cost, and hence fixed for any course, for most one-way technologies currently used in autonomous distance teaching institutions, fixed costs usually far exceed variable costs. This means that the economies of scale apply to one-way technologies: the more students, the more cost-effective these technologies become.
>
> Two-way technologies, such as audio and computer conferencing, reduce the fixed costs, but have high variable costs. Thus, while suitable for courses with relatively low student numbers, they will be increasingly expensive for courses with large student numbers.
>
> *(Bates, 1995: 6)*

The problem with high technology–constructivist courses is that they contain both elements: they have the high production costs traditionally found with one-way technologies such as print and television, but also the high variable costs associated with two-way technologies, without the payback of reduced fixed costs Bates mentions. Such courses thus represent a fundamental shift in the traditional distance education economic model. Maintaining a balance between these two elements will prove to be the key factor in successfully developing and delivering such courses.

A case study

Examining the course I know best, namely T171, in the light of the framework above, enables some of the considerations relating to technology, pedagogy and costs to be explored further.

Technology

T171 consists of a large Web site (over 800 pages), and an associated CMC environment. The Web site is implemented in HTML (although it is now stored in XML, with content and style separated, students see it as standard HTML pages). Incorporated within the Web site are around 10 professionally designed animations, implemented in Flash. There are also a great many images, and some small video clips. The conferencing is realized through a system called FirstClass by Centrinity, which is used across the university. Students can access this via a Web browser interface or through a client. The Web site has links that go directly to conferences, so for example students might be prompted to discuss an issue, or seek help during an activity in a particular conference set up for this purpose.

Navigation is quite linear, with a 'Where next' box at the foot of each page. Students can navigate via index pages, or a study calendar. When they click a 'Done' button at the foot of each page their progress is recorded and displayed on a visual course map, so they can gain a sense of their individual progress through the material.

Some of these features, such as the visual navigation aid, the videos and a redesign of the Web site, were implemented in the fourth presentation of the course. This illustrates another issue related to online courses: that they are in a constant state of development. The Web design, which had looked modern in 1999, looked dated in 2002 and so it was redone.

Some of the decisions regarding technology were made through expediency. For example, it made sense to use the FirstClass conferencing environment, since this was widely known and supported through the university, and it matched our needs. Other decisions were made to suit the technical demands of the students. Most students would be accessing the course via a home PC and modem, probably at speeds of 56K. This limits the type of media that the course can use. Video is poor with such bandwidth, and so it could not be used extensively. We implemented some in the later version of the course, but it represented non-essential elements. For example, there is a clip of Donald Davies explaining the concept of packet switching, which helps to bring the idea alive, but the key content has been covered in the text.

We also considered the level of students and their experience with the medium. T171 is a level one course, which means that many of the students might not have studied at this level before, or might be returning to study after a long break. The course was aimed at a broad audience and was intended as an introduction to information technologies and the issues associated with them. Many of the students therefore were unfamiliar with using the Web and computer conferencing. For this reason we adopted a simple navigation structure and kept additional technology to a minimum. Incorporating different forms of software, even standard plug-ins, always introduces an element of unpredictability. A small proportion of students will have difficulties in getting these to work, but on a course with a large student cohort this can represent a significant number of students. So we tried to maintain a balance between robustness and interesting use of media.

For these reasons I would say that T171 is probably somewhere in the middle along the technology axis. It is more than a standard set of pages and a bulletin board, but equally there are a lot of technologies and functions it does not employ.

This illustrates that it is not always the case that more technology is better. Some of the reasons we did not employ certain technologies arose from valid considerations regarding the level and access of students and the scale of the course. Of course, one can always implement more, and T171 will continue to develop.

Pedagogy

The approach in T171 is that much of the teaching is done via narrative (Weller, 2000b). Students have a set book for each module, which covers the story of how the PC or the Internet was developed, for example. The Web site then carries wrap-around academic material, exploring issues and concepts raised in the book, explaining some technologies in greater detail and providing material that is not covered by the book. Combined with this is a strong emphasis on group work and discussion. There are a number of group activities in each of the three modules, which relate directly to the assessment of the course. In addition, students are directed to discuss issues raised by the course in specific conferences. Guest speakers, for example the authors of the set texts, are also invited in to the conferences to answer student questions, and this is used to provoke debate. At the end of the course students are required to construct a portfolio that consists of elements such as exercises from the modules and exchanges in conferences. They are asked to reflect and analyse these, so participation is encouraged throughout the course.

In some respects the pedagogy of T171 is a reasonably straightforward didactic approach. Concepts are explained through a variety of media, then students are tested on that understanding. The course also incorporates constructivist elements, however. The use of collaborative exercises, the emphasis on dialogue and assessment based around reflection and portfolio are all strong constructivist methods.

So, as with technology, I would place T171 in the middle of the didactic–constructivist axis. This demonstrates that it is possible to have a mixture of approaches in a course design, and it is not necessarily a case of choosing one approach over another.

As with technology, our decisions regarding the pedagogy were based on our perception of what would work best with these students and meet the objectives of the course. As mentioned above, many T171 students are new to distance learning and also new to the medium. It would thus be an additional factor to introduce them to a learning style which was different from anything they had experienced previously. Many students are somewhat nervous and apprehensive about returning to study, so it is important that they feel they have done all that is required of them. In this sense a didactic approach is more reassuring, since the necessary tasks can be specified clearly. A constructivist approach is more open-ended and at the discretion of the student. It is therefore perhaps better suited to more experienced learners. The clear, linear navigation through the Web site was another realization of this concern about demands upon students. Students more experienced with the medium and with studying might find a less linear structure and a more resource-based approach suitable.

However, we wanted to utilize the Net to its full advantage, and part of the course objectives was to give students an appreciation of how the Net can be used – as I mentioned in a previous chapter, the medium is the message. Group work and discussion were therefore key elements in the course philosophy.

Issues of scale

When you are dealing with large-scale courses a number of issues arise which are felt more profoundly with online delivery. If constructivist elements are being incorporated into the course, then there is the need for intimate, small-scale interactions between students and with an educator. This is contrasted with the need to deliver a course to a large number of students, ensuring it is robust and manageable. This tension between industrial and intimate scales requires the course designers to develop procedures that suit the needs of both.

On a large-scale course, it is not possible for a single educator to provide all of the support. There is a need for more focused educator support on a much smaller scale. The part-time tutor model adopted by many distance education establishments is one such solution. Each tutor is assigned a number of students, for whom he or she provides support, marks assessments and runs activities. The main course, however, is designed by a different team of educators, so it is not the tutor's task to teach the subject from scratch, but rather to provide support within the framework of the course. The use of such part-time staff solves one set of issues, but raises another, namely that of tutor support and development. This may be particularly germane with online courses, where many tutors will need support in effective online moderating, technical issues and teaching at a distance. There are two components to such support: that which occurs prior to the course start, and ongoing support throughout the course. The development of generic tutor support material for effective online tutoring is a matter the institution as a whole should take up. Offering ongoing support is also vital to the success of a large-scale online course. The nature of the medium encourages communication and queries, so the course developers will receive far more requests than they might have done with traditional distance education courses. These will be from both students and tutors. It is important therefore to implement systems that enable these queries to be dealt with quickly, but also prevent the course developers from being overwhelmed.

The student conference structure on T171 was outlined in Chapter 6. In addition to these student conferences, there is a similar structure for tutor support, incorporating technical issues, an educational discussion forum, several resources and FAQs, as well as a read-only noticeboard. This structure is shown in Figure 10.2. Some of these conferences are moderated by experienced tutors, to whom an additional fee is paid. Each of these moderators can bring queries to a higher level conference, where the course team can deal with them. This filtering of queries is essential in coping with the scale of such a course (Robinson and Weller 2002).

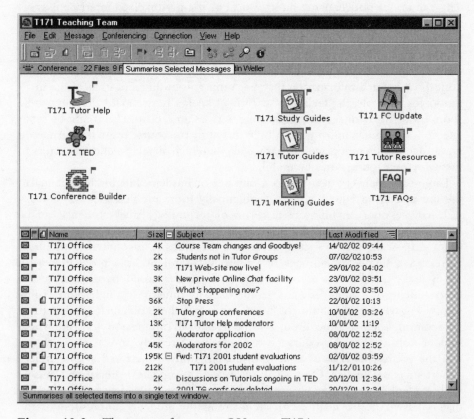

Figure 10.2 *The tutor conferences on OU course T171*

In addition, there is a good deal of tutor support material. This includes specifications for activities, including sample e-mails, guidance on how to deal with certain issues that may arise, suggested timetables for activities and so forth. These are sent to tutors at the appropriate time during the course. Tutors also receive more general advice regarding issues that may be affecting their students and how to deal with them: for instance, how to welcome students at the start of the course, advising students on the choice of their next course at the mid-point, and helping students as they come towards the end of the course.

With the asynchronous nature of communication on the Net, tutors will feel engaged in an ongoing dialogue with their students. Unlike courses that may have regularly arranged face to face tutorials, the online course does not have any gaps between student contact. Therefore it is important for the course developers to support tutors throughout the course.

It is also necessary to develop efficient means of disseminating information. This can be via noticeboards, direct e-mail or if a personalized interface is available, by students opting in to information services. Just as the amount of information coming back to course developers is increased through the use of the Net, so the flow outward increases also. It is essential that students and tutors know where to find important information. These can be in the form of FAQs, conferences or noticeboards. Such information may be coming from different parts of the institution: for example, the technical staff might keep a noticeboard alerting people about problems with servers, downtimes, viruses and so on. This might be separate from the course information disseminated by the course team. If information is available in different places, an early exercise which alerts students and tutors to these different sources may be useful.

Large-scale delivery also brings a number of burdens. For instance, it makes the use of cutting edge technology potentially more problematic. On a small-scale course one can innovate in terms of technology, since students can be offered more support, and the number of problems will be comparatively few. On a large-scale course a small percentage of students encountering problems represents a significant number of people. What might be a problem with a set-up for a single student on a small-scale course could translate into 100 or so students on a large-scale course, and the part-time tutors might not be sufficiently knowledgeable about the technicalities of the problem to deal with it. In addition, such a large group would create an impression for the whole student cohort that the course was unreliable. Similarly, the need to ensure that the course material is stable and unambiguous is increased as the student cohort increases in size. On a small scale one can update material and engage with students on a more personal basis. With large-scale delivery the course material itself is the main factor in forming the students' impression of the course.

The key issue with large-scale delivery of online courses is that it involves developing new procedures and approaches. These invariably involve new costs, so the notion that online courses can lead to large-scale delivery at relatively low cost is a mistaken one. It is based on the view that digital resources are unaffected by the number of users. While this is true, it is also the case that as the scale increases, so does the need for people to act in intermediary roles in order to maintain a suitable educational environment.

Lessons for implementation

1   Determine the audience for the course and develop the course accordingly

A course aimed at busy professionals may well differ in approach and technology from one aimed at full-time students. The former might be richer in its mix of technology and adopt a clear, didactic approach. The latter might utilize less technology but focus on student exploration and discussion. This is one obvious way in which the audience for a course can influence its design. Other factors that need to be considered are the technological awareness of students and educators, the learning experience of the potential students, the suitability of the topic to a particular approach or technology, the existence of technology or media that can easily be incorporated or adapted for use in a course and the level of technical support available during development and presentation.

2   Determine the presentation and production costs and allocate resources accordingly

When a new function or a new piece of technology is demonstrated, many educators become strangers to restraint – they simply have to find a way to include it in a course. This is particularly true for online courses, where the technology plays such a dominant role in the student experience. This 'barnacle' model of course production, where each successive technology is added on to the existing course without any reduction, is to be avoided for two reasons. The first is that it increases the production load for the course. The second is that it adds to the student workload. It is important to maintain a sense of currency on online courses and avoid them looking dated. However, if new technology is included whose use is going to require a significant amount of time from students (and the time taken to interact with technology can often be hard to estimate), then it needs to be at the expense of other material.

Similarly, if a constructivist method such as collaborative work, resource searching or active discussion is implemented, this cannot be in addition to a large quantity of didactic material. These activities are notoriously time-consuming, so suitable 'space' within the course needs to be created for students to engage in them successfully.

The potential risks in adopting a course strategy that requires high production and presentation costs have been outlined. These risks will require educators to make sometimes painful decisions, since they may not be able to have all the elements in a course they feel it requires.

There also needs to be an appreciation and commitment from the institution of the need for support for educators during presentation. A low technology–constructivist course may be produced in a relatively short timescale, but the educator is likely to be heavily involved during the presentation of such a course.

3   Appreciate the influence of the scale of presentation

If you are developing a course that is likely to have a small-scale presentation, say less than 50 students per year, then this has some advantages and disadvantages. The main advantage is that it allows the educator to offer a good deal of support to students. This means that the course can be innovative in pedagogy and technology. The disadvantage is that such a course cannot afford to spend a great deal on the development of expensive technology or media. For such courses, using a Web delivery system such as the ones outlined in the previous chapter represents a cost-efficient method of producing a course that contains a number of advanced technical elements.

If the course is large scale, say 1,000 students or over, then the course developers need to implement the sort of systems for dealing with scale outlined above. Educators in this case need to appreciate that much of their energy will be devoted to the management of the overall course and its various systems rather than to direct student interaction. Institutions need to appreciate the need for such information management and delegation structures and the corresponding costs associated with these.

For medium-scale courses a delicate balance needs to be struck between the two. They rapidly move beyond the capability of a single educator, so there is a need for other staff members, either full or part-time, to support the course. This can be difficult for educators, as such courses may struggle to maintain the closeness of contact achieved on a small-scale course and yet not have the structures in place found on a large-scale one.

Conclusion

The framework outlined here incorporates the two main influences in an online course, namely pedagogy and technology. This provides four broad categories of online courses, which match many of the current offerings. Examining each category allows the educator to address issues relating to the cost of production and presentation of an online course. Acknowledging these different aspects of cost and demands of different course types will be an important factor in how well organizations adapt to providing online education.

In the next chapter we will look at some current trends which will have an impact on the way online learning develops over the coming years. We will also look at an analogous situation in another industry.

Summary

In this chapter I have outlined a framework for classifying online courses. Each course can be categorized according to where it falls on a low–high technology axis and a didactic–constructivist pedagogy axis. Using this framework the issues associated with the following four categories of course were discussed:

● high technology – didactic;
● low technology – didactic;
● low technology – constructivist;
● high technology – constructivist.

Using this framework the Open University course T171 was then examined in terms of its pedagogy, technology and issues relating to the scale of the course presentation. From this, three lessons for implementation were drawn:

● Determine the audience for the course and develop the course accordingly.
● Determine the presentation and production costs and allocate resources accordingly.
● Appreciate the influence of the scale of presentation.

Chapter 11

Birth of the new

Introduction

This book has had two main threads: the implications of the Internet as an educational tool and the issues to consider when implementing an online course. As with technology and pedagogy, I believe it is impossible to dissociate these two elements. The ways in which individuals or institutions implement online learning will be profoundly affected by the views they hold about its potential, the changing educational environment, the student audience, the best use of the technology and the role of education within society. In turn, the way in which online courses are implemented helps shape these views. It is difficult for people to retain reservations or opposition in the face of success and evident student satisfaction. On the other hand, poor results will seem to readily back up many negative views.

   Online education now enters its most significant stage, when it will move into the mainstream of education and perhaps challenge the traditional modes of teaching. Some of the issues that will have a profound effect on how this is realized are examined in this chapter. The recurrent themes in the book will also be drawn out. First, we will look at the situation that arose with regard to home video and the cinema, which is somewhat analogous to the one that education is currently in, and see what lessons may be learnt.

Video and cinema

The penetration of video players as a household commodity really became significant in the early 1980s. This saw the rise of a new industry, that of home video rental of cinema releases. Many observers predicted that this would be detrimental to cinema, or even bring about its demise. This fear seemed to be confirmed when cinema attendance fell during the 1980s, reaching a low in the EU of around 577 million, compared with the peak of 4,058 million in 1955 (Deiss, 2002). However, major film producers soon realized that home video represented a significant additional source of income. For example, Ronald Davis (1997) states that 'in 1986 more than half the domestic revenue earned by major studios came from videocassette sales and rentals. Warner's blockbuster *Batman*, for instance, grossed $250 million within its first five months of theatrical release; when the picture was released on video, it earned $400 million.' Viewing film on home video has obvious advantages – many people find it difficult to get to cinemas, or miss a film during its release, or their local cinema does not show their choice of film. Video offers convenience, it can be rented from almost anywhere (newsagents, garages, corner shops, etc) and viewed at home at anytime on relatively inexpensive equipment.

Yet the home video did not mean the death of cinema. Since that low in the 1980s cinema attendance has been increasing. The 1990s saw a reversal in the process of decline that had been in progress since the 1950s. In the EU admissions rose by some 47 per cent between 1990 and 2000, reaching 850 million cinema visits in 2000 (Deiss, 2002).

So both industries have prospered alongside each other. How is this so? There are several reasons, some of which relate to general prosperity and changing leisure habits. But it is also the case that the home video industry, far from being damaging to the film industry, actually turned out to be a beneficial force. Watching movies was not a zero-sum game. The home video market generated an interest in films in general, which was manifested in rising cinema attendance. The arrival of video also made the cinema industry go through a process of reappraisal. In order to compete with the convenience of home viewing it needed to make a virtue of what it could offer – namely, more of a leisure experience. So cinemas became large out-of-town multiplexes that incorporated bars, restaurants and other leisure activities, and offered convenient parking. This made going to the cinema much more of a social occasion suited to modern leisure habits. While we might mourn the decline of the art deco cinemas situated in town centres, the multiplexes have been responsible for a change in the perception of cinema attendance. In conjunction with this, film studios produced films that suited the multiplexes, such as blockbusters, which benefit from the large screen and appeal to a wide audience.

There are parallels here with online and campus education. Online education, like home video, offers convenience for many people – it removes many of the spatial and temporal constraints inherent in the activity. As with the established industry's early reaction to home video, many universities perceive online education as a threat. However, it is likely that, as with video and cinema, the two can be mutually beneficial. The Net allows people to participate in education who might otherwise be excluded. Having studied once, these people may later study with a campus university, or the Net may be the means through which the campus university reaches them. Students may find a mixed approach beneficial, studying partly online at a distance and spending some periods attending a campus. The lifelong learning market indicates that the need for ongoing education will be substantial: as with film, it is not a zero-sum market, in that people do not only have one encounter with higher education. In addition, many universities are struggling to cope with the expansion required to physically accommodate many students. Online education offers an alternative to this, which suits the needs of both students and universities.

As with any analogy there is some degree of mismatch and some elements do not map across. For instance, films that are produced direct for the video market are usually of lesser quality than films that receive a cinema release. There is no evidence or reason to suggest that courses that are produced solely for the online market will be inferior to campus based courses. Indeed, the reverse is probably true with regard to education, in that courses that were designed for campus delivery do not work well when transferred to the new medium, whereas courses designed specifically to be delivered online can compete in terms of educational quality with campus courses.

However, there are sufficient similarities between the two stories for the case of the film industry to be instructive. As with cinemas, it may be the case that universities have to undergo a change in their operation and image in order to compete effectively with the upstart industry and incorporate the impact it has upon the established mode of operation. If this is achieved, the two can develop and maintain a symbiotic relationship.

Future issues

Having a section that looks at possible future trends is of course a notoriously foolhardy thing to do. Not only does the technology change rapidly, but so do people's attitudes towards it. What was once seen as a promising technology becomes superseded by a new one. As I have mentioned, books in the early 1990s were full of the promise of CD ROM, and before that CAL and artificial intelligence tools were the focus of attention. As we have seen, the Net has instigated something of a renewed interest, or some might say a change in direction for many of these topics. The Net itself will undergo such change, but what is likely to remain is the emphasis on communication. After the Net, educational technology will never be so isolated again. Rather than attempt to predict what technologies will arise or the way universities will look a hundred years from now, the focus is on some current issues and technologies that will become increasingly important over the next few years and will shape the way online learning is delivered.

Intellectual property

This is a huge topic, one far beyond the scope of this book. It concerns legal, artistic, moral, commercial and technical issues, all of which have very detailed arguments. For this reason it is often hard to determine exactly what the impact will be in educational terms. It is an area that has many of the Net intelligentsia seriously concerned. Samuelson (1996), commenting on the US Government's White Paper *Intellectual Property and the National Information Infrastructure*, claims that 'your traditional user rights to browse, share, or make private noncommercial copies of copyrighted works will be rescinded. Not only that, your online service provider will be forced to snoop through your files, ready to cut you off and turn you in if it finds any unlicensed material there.' It is this shift from protecting the public, commercial use of material to controlling private, non-commercial use that is causing concern. As with much of the way we perform education, existing copyright has a lot to do with the physicality of a product. It is the ease of perfect electronic reproduction that worries commercial organizations.

The issue at the heart of intellectual property and the Net is to what extent the Net is just the same as any other medium. There are those who contest that the existing copyright laws are sufficient, and there is nothing substantially different about the Net. There are others who argue that the Net is different in significant ways, and new copyright laws need to be introduced, or new measures need to be implemented, to protect existing freedoms. This returns us to the notion of the Net as a place of paradox. To what extent is it just an extension of existing behaviour, and to what extent does it facilitate new behaviours? Here are some reasons why people suggest the Net is different with regards to copyright:

- Ease of monitoring. Because it is easy to trace the content you look at when online, your ISP could keep track of everything you read, view or browse (although this would involve additional costs for them). This would have involved high levels of surveillance before, but software allows it to be easily achieved when online. Once it becomes a practical possibility, the view of existing laws shifts. Maybe the government did have the right to spy on people before, or open mail if it thought it suspicious, but that was unlikely for most of us. If it can now be done easily, to what extent do our civil liberties need protecting even further?
- Ill-matching metaphors. As I have mentioned before, on the Net one often struggles to find an analogous situation in real life. The same applies with copyright and civil liberties on the Net. Are hackers simply breaking the law, or are they striking a blow for individual freedom? If people break a US law, but are living in Russia when they do it, where there is no such law, should they be arrested in the United States? This happened famously with the case of Sklyarov, who wrote a program that broke the security codes of Adobe's e-book reader and was promptly arrested when in Las Vegas. Trying to apply existing laws to the Net without taking into consideration the nature of the medium or the culture it espouses can sometimes lead to awkward

prosecutions or even potentially damaging conclusions. For example, the idea that viewing a Web page involved making a copy in your computer's RAM and therefore infringed copyright was once put forward, which would have threatened the entire Web. Jessica Litman (2000) has argued that the Net is implicated at the level of the electron according to existing copyright laws.

- Ill-informed decision makers. One of the problems is that a field that involves advanced technical arguments about what is and what is not feasible is often difficult for non-experts to understand. In the case of legislation and the Net, the people who make the important decisions are judges and politicians, often with very little understanding of the topic. They can make rulings based on the pressures applied by commercial organizations or on knee-jerk reactions to public outcries. For example, in the UK there was a case in 2000 where a British-based couple adopted a baby from the United States via the Internet. There was, quite rightly, much public concern about a trade in babies being developed. Some politicians suggested that such Web sites should be banned, so that UK citizens could not view them. Although such a law did not come into force, the suggestion itself demonstrates a considerable lack of understanding of both how the Internet actually works and also the civil liberty implications in enforcing such a control over the material citizens can read.
- Ease of distribution. The very success of the Net is based on the ease of publishing and distributing material. No longer bound by the need for physical copies of material, it means copies can be distributed quickly, so as computer viruses demonstrate, a single entity can proliferate globally almost overnight. This is a publisher's worst nightmare. Trying to chase after copies once they have begun to spread is almost impossible, and it is difficult to locate and prosecute the original perpetrator. For this reason many publishers feel that new powers are required to protect the intellectual property of works.
- The culture of the Net. Freedom of speech and open access have long been the accepted values of the Net culture. It is based around a right to publish freely and allow users free access to material. Once the commercial forces began to arrive on the Net there was always going to be a clash of values. For many Net enthusiasts any attempt to restrict these freedoms is a fundamental attack on the values of their culture.

All of these issues may concern us as individuals, but what direct influence do they have on education? One significant way in which they could affect education is by directly controlling activities at the very heart of education. Richard Stallman (1997) talks about the 'right to read', and suggests that if commercial companies control passwords (as many fear Microsoft's Passport technology will do) and ISPs monitor usage, then every time you read a piece of material it must be paid for. The digital equivalent of loaning a book to a friend becomes an infringement of copyright. Obviously, any legislation or technology that controls reading would have an impact on students and educators. Similarly such legislation could affect the research and publication activities of educators.

Another possible impact of a ruling that requires users to be monitored is that it places an emphasis on universities themselves to monitor and control student behaviour. Many universities act as the ISP for their students, or the students will be using the university's network for study. If the legislation requires ISPs to monitor their users and indeed be held responsible for their behaviour, then universities will find themselves in the position of having to enforce very strict codes of conduct. For example in December 2001 the FBI raided several universities including MIT and UCLA, in an attempt to break a software piracy ring comprising students and employees (*New York Times*, 12 December 2001 – http://www.nytimes.com/2001/12/12/technology/12PIRA. html).

The issues surrounding intellectual property seem to bring the liberties of users in direct conflict with the commercial interests of large corporations, so the debate can be highly charged. There are those who feel that large corporations are going to gain control of every aspect of the Net and need to be resisted through new legislation. And there are those who feel that current copyright laws are quite adequate if applied properly. My personal view, and this is by no means my area of expertise, is that these issues will tend to sort themselves out. There is simply no point in having the capability to charge everyone for looking at your pages if people stop looking at them and go to a competitor's site that offers free content. We have seen many predictions of potential world domination and control, but they always failed to materialize (unless you believe conspiracy theories), mainly because people opt to go elsewhere. However, the whole area of copyright and intellectual property is one with which educators and institutions in particular need to maintain a familiarity.

The underlying question is to what extent will knowledge, previously freely available, become privatized? If it does become privatized this has serious implications for the way in which all education, but particularly online education, is conducted.

Broadband

Broadband is usually defined as being an 'always-on' connection, with speeds of over 500 kilobytes per second (KPS) and carrying different types of media. It is commonly available in homes via cable modems, which use the same cable as the television companies, or through ADSL (asymmetric digital subscriber line), which uses existing telephone wires. The transmission rates can vary depending on the technology and the provider. It also depends on what you wish to use broadband for. There is something of a trade-off between upload and download speeds. If the broadband is mainly for delivery of content, for example video on demand, then it makes sense to use most of the bandwidth on download speeds, of say 7 megabytes per second. If it is being used for video conferencing, for example, then the upload and download speeds need to be equal, say around 600 KPS.

Broadband is already commonplace in many areas, so it hardly qualifies as a future technology. Its penetration is likely to increase, however, and costs are set to fall. If distance educators can assume all users have broadband, then that alters greatly the sophistication they can employ in media. Streaming video is no longer problematic, and synchronous working packages incorporating good-quality video conferencing, shared work areas and instantaneous transmission of documents will become commonplace. This will have an impact on how an online course is supposed to look and feel. There is a danger here that the temptation then is to assume that it is the same as face to face education, and as has been stressed throughout this book, this is not necessarily the case, even with high bandwidths. Some of the access advantages of text and asynchronous communication may be lost in the excitement of broadband.

It will take some time for most online courses to move to a solely broadband platform, and even longer to fully take advantage of the medium. Initially it will mean less concern about image intensive Web sites (not good news for partially sighted users), greater use of synchronous working tools and an increase in the use of video. All this is not exactly a change in kind of the online course, just more of the same, and delivered more reliably.

Perhaps what will be most interesting about broadband will be the way in which it changes the perception of online education. There is something of a barrier to online study for many people. If students have metered access, then the cost of being online, even if they can claim it back, creates a psychological pressure – a clock ticking away which is detrimental to study. The provision of unmetered access, whereby the amount of time online is irrelevant once a flat monthly fee is paid, alleviates some of this pressure. There is still the concern of occupying a telephone line (particularly if it is the only one in the household), and even just the effort of dialling up or the frustration of waiting for pages to download. Broadband will go a significant way to altering people's attitude towards their use of the Net. A high-speed connection that is always on and is unmetered means people will use the Net more frequently. Once broadband becomes the norm in most homes, the Net will function in the manner many of us like to pretend it does already. This speed and reliability could well bring about the mass breakthrough for online education.

Success of e-commerce

I have already mentioned that e-commerce is a few years in advance of education in the lessons it has learnt about online delivery. Following the collapse of the e-commerce boom and the fall in share prices, much of the initial optimism surrounding e-commerce has dissipated. The way in which e-commerce develops in this more realistic climate will have an influence on the way in which successful online education is delivered. If the market for all online products grows, then the demand for education delivered in the same format will follow suit. This may see the arrival of new commercial entities in the education market that compete seriously with universities. If there is a backlash against solely online companies, and the Net becomes simply another outlet for established organizations, then the same may happen in education. Existing universities will offer some online programmes, but these will often remain secondary to their primary market – the campus based student. The current market tends to favour the latter approach, as students seem reluctant to sign up with online-only universities, preferring established providers. After the initial hype a subsequent backlash was always likely, but use of the Net will continue to rise steadily over the next few years, and with it the demand for online education. It may not be the overnight force of change many predicted, but it will establish a large market.

Another issue relating to e-commerce is the success or otherwise of the financial models adopted online. The portal model, whereby a site acts as a central broker for other sites and makes its money through advertising and affiliation contracts, was hailed as the new financial model for the Net. This was due to the success of portals such as Yahoo. Recently, however, this model has become less profitable, and many e-commerce start-ups have found that it is simply not viable. This has seen a return to more traditional models based around the sale of a product. The portal model has attracted much interest in the area of education, with many online education companies effectively acting as brokers for courses provided at separate institutions. If the portal model of e-commerce does prove to be ultimately unsuccessful, this may have an effect on the future direction of online education.

The general downfall in fortunes of e-commerce companies has created a reluctance to invest in online education ventures, but it still remains an area of keen interest for many venture capitalists. In many ways education represents a much more reliable online market than many of the e-commerce start-ups. It is a product that is ideally suited to online delivery, and the online version offers distinct advantages for a certain audience.

It is probably the relationship between universities and commercial organizations, whether they provide technical support, content, or a ready market, that will be the most significant in shaping the online education arena. The Net brings these two forces together in teaching in a way that has previously only been seen in research.

Learning technology standards

In Chapter 7 I mentioned the development of standards associated with learning objects. The basic idea behind learning objects is that they represent reusable pieces of information that can be implemented in different courses, on different platforms. Currently the granularity for educational objects is the course itself, and there are many cases of courses being shared or adapted for implementation elsewhere. However, the course is too large an item for efficient sharing. There are too many differences between local needs, level of students, where the course fits in a curriculum and so on. A finer granularity is required, and this is the learning object. There is still some debate as to what exactly constitutes a learning object: for example, if you have an image in a page explaining analogue signals, say, then is the overall page the learning object or do the text and the image constitute separate objects? Let us for now assume a learning object is some piece of educational media (text, image, video, audio, presentation, or combination of these) which explains a single concept, idea, fact or process.

Learning objects are non-proprietary: that is, they can be implemented in any learning management system (LMS). In reality this means they are specified in terms of XML, with associated metadata, which we have looked at already. There are several advantages to having content in this form:

- Portability – separating content from proprietary systems allows material to be used in different places and in different systems.
- Content management – having content as separate objects facilitates searching and management of a large resource. It also allows easy updating, since only single objects have to be changed, even if these are used in multiple courses.
- Course production – all over the world educators are explaining the same concepts. Instead of creating multiple versions of the same content, learning objects can be incorporated from elsewhere. Creating entire courses from scratch is expensive, and reusable content offers a means of alleviating this.
- Customization – institutions can easily insert objects into a customized system, or adapt the object itself to suit their needs.

In order for this to be achieved the technology needs to support the standards. Currently the IEEE, IMS and US Defense Department are all involved in the development of specifications.

It is unlikely that courses will be created entirely from third party learning objects. Adding material and creating a framework within which the content makes sense will still be necessary. The use of learning objects to cover standard material can allow the educator to focus on tasks such as student support.

At the moment most LMS manufacturers offer compliance with the e-learning specifications put forward by the various bodies. However, their systems still provide proprietary functionality, and it is often this functionality which adds the most to a course. So it could be the case that a course has both proprietary and non-proprietary elements, making adaptation a difficult process.

These specifications will be modified in the light of use, and there will be a move towards consensus between the differing bodies over the next few years. The possible benefits of a world where learning objects are the norm are great, but actually arriving at that stage may be a difficult and time-consuming process. For an educator it requires a significant change in the way material is produced, and also a great deal of effort to tag each learning object with the appropriate metadata. When there is pressure to create a course quickly, then the short-term gains in producing specific linear course material may outweigh the potential benefits of producing generic, granular objects.

The idea of material reuse has been around for a long time, and yet it still has not really had any impact on course development. It represents something of a Holy Grail in e-learning, and there is no doubt that the technology now makes it a much more tangible Grail. Whether it is achieved will depend largely on the efforts of educators and institutions to make it a reality. This will be one of the most significant areas to watch over the next few years, since it could radically alter how online courses are developed and who develops them.

The course of the future

What will online courses be like in the near future? Taking into account all that we have covered in this book, let us bring it together in one hypothetical course.

The course is 'Looking at Shakespeare', an undergraduate course which looks at five Shakespeare plays and addresses issues such as the role of women in Shakespeare, the nature of interpretation, the social context in which they were written and the significance of power in the plays. The course is offered by the Global E-University, a private online-only university which has contracts with major universities to provide content and accreditation. The course can be studied by anyone in any country, either as part of a Global E-University degree or for credit points that are recognized at all the main universities.

The course was created by using learning objects collected from a pool of Shakespeare resources as well as some material developed specifically for this course. Some of the learning objects were free and the rights to others were purchased. The course components include:

- video and audio of productions of the plays;
- a virtual stage where students can collaboratively direct a play;
- annotated versions of the texts, to which students can add their own notes;
- a live video lecture from a respected Shakespearean critic, with a subsequent question and answer session;
- a database of articles relating to the plays and subjects;
- asynchronous discussion conferences;
- video conferencing facilities for group discussions;
- a personalized interface where students can store notes, be notified of important information and register for discussion groups of their choice;
- an intelligent tracking system which monitors student behaviour and identifies potential problems, which the tutor is notified about;
- an intelligent help system which answers real language queries regarding technical help, general university policy and study skills advice;

● a Web site which provides specially authored material and acts as the framework combining all of the above elements, which can be viewed on different
platforms, such as a PC, e-books and PDAs (personal digital assistants).

The course is offered in different languages, with different versions of each
learning object available, so the Web site is created dynamically once a student
selects their preferred language.

Students can sign up for the course at any stage of the year; they are not
restricted to term times. When there are sufficient student numbers within that
language set for a tutor group, the part-time tutor is notified and the students are
automatically allocated to the appropriate tutor conference. The Web site is available all the time, but for the students the course runs when there is a tutor group
ready to go. At any one time there will be different tutor groups at different stages
through the course.

There is both an independent study and a collaborative element to the course.
Students are expected to direct a virtual performance of the play by working in
groups, role-play different characters under hypothetical circumstances, work
towards a group goal by sharing knowledge they have found from the resource
base and peer assess each other's essays. They also work individually, compiling
and analysing a set of resources, writing an essay, critically analysing a performance of the play and studying a range of resources. The assessment reinforces
this approach, providing marks for the overall virtual play direction, analysis of the
role-playing exercise, the comments provided in the peer review exercise, as well
as for the individual pieces of work.

All these elements are feasible now: this course is no piece of science fiction
(indeed, many will think it is rather limited in its ambitions). There may well be
courses in existence which would claim all of these features. This represents the
major drive over the next few years in online education – the stabilization of
online courses, rather than radical leaps forward. What will be remarkable is not
what is possible at the cutting edge of technology where only a few interested
parties are working, but rather that such courses as the one outlined above will
become the norm for a great many students. Then, when we look back it will be
apparent that we have witnessed the birth of a new form of education.

Conclusion

The Net raises many new issues, and the difficulty is often deciding to what
extent these require a completely new way of operating, or whether existing
procedures can be adapted. As the example of the home video and cinema industries demonstrates, there are similarities with other areas, and yet there are also
significant differences. This is felt keenly in areas such as intellectual property,
where the sudden rise in connectivity changes the scale of the problem. It is this
connectivity that also makes any potential changes in legislation so worrying,

since it is difficult to isolate and control one form of behaviour in a connected society without also affecting other, legitimate behaviours.

The general success of e-commerce, broadband uptake and educational projects such as learning object standards will go a long way to shape online education over the next few years. The degree to which commercial organizations and regulators of the Net come to control what it is used for and who uses it may also determine the nature of e-learning. Ultimately I hope that it will be influenced by two interested parties: the students, particularly those of the next generation who have grown up online as it were, and the educators who begin to fashion something new, appropriate and most of all exciting in this medium.

Summary

This final chapter has addressed a number of different issues, including:

- The home video and cinema industries as an analogy to online and campus based education.
- Future issues which will influence the direction online education takes in the coming years. These included intellectual property, the rise of broadband access, the success of e-commerce operations and the development of learning technology standards.
- A hypothetical course of the future that draws on the content covered in this book.

References

Adams, P C (1998) Teaching and learning with SimCity 2000, *Journal of Geography*, **97** (2), pp 47–55

Albert, S and Thomas, C (2000) A new approach to computer-aided learning: the automated tutor, *Open Learning*, **15** (2), pp 141–50

Alexander, G (1998) Communication and collaboration on-line: new course models at the Open University, presented at the Networked Life-long Learning Conference, Sheffield University, Sheffield, 20–22 April 1998 [On-line] http://sustainability.open.ac.uk/gary/onlinelearn/ [Accessed November 2001]

Alexander, S (1999) Selection, dissemination and evaluation of the TopClass WWW-based course support tool, *International Journal of Educational Tele-communications*, **5** (4), pp 283–92

Baiocchi, O, Landrum, J, Olson, J and Olson, N (1999) Evolution of a web course: a case study, in *Proceedings of Advances in Multimedia and Distance Education Symposium ISIMADE 99*, Baden-Baden, Germany, August 1999, ed M R Syed, O Baiocchi and G E Lasker, International Institute for Advanced Studies in Systems Research and Cybernetics

Bates, A W (1995) *Technology, Open Learning and Distance Education*, Routledge, London

Borges, J L (1964) *Labyrinths*, Penguin, London

Boud, D (ed) (1988) *Developing Student Autonomy in Learning*, Kogan Page, London

Boyd, H and Cowan, J (1985) A case for self-assessment based on recent studies of student learning, *Assessment and Evaluation in Higher Education*, **10** (3), pp 225–35

Brown, J S, Collins, A and Duguid, P (1989) Situated cognition and the culture of learning, *Educational Researcher*, **18** (1), pp 32–42 [Online] http://www.slofi.com/situated.htm [Accessed September 2001]

Chang, C (2001) Construction and evaluation of a Web-based learning portfolio system: an electronic assessment tool, *Innovations in Education and Teaching International*, **38** (2), pp 144–55

Christensen, C M (1997) *The Innovator's Dilemma:When new technologies cause great firms to fail*, Harvard Business School Press, Boston, Mass.

Collis, B, De Boer, W and Slotman, K (2001) Feedback for web-based assignments, *Journal of Computer Assisted Learning*, **17** (3), pp 306–13

Daniel, J S (2000) The Internet and higher education: preparing for change, address at the Internet Revolution Conference, London, 9 May 2000 [Online] http://www.open.ac.uk. [Accessed December 2001]

Davis, R L (1997) *Celluloid Mirrors: Hollywood and American society since 1945*, Harcourt Brace College, Fort Worth, USA

Dede, C (1996) The evolution of constructivist learning environments: immersion in distributed, virtual worlds, in *Constructivist Learning Environments: Case studies in instructional design*, ed B G Wilson, pp 165–75, Educational Technology, New Jersey, USA

Deiss, R (2002) *Statistics in Focus: Cinema statistics – growth in cinema going continues in 2000 and 2001*, Theme 4: 4/2002, Eurostat [Online] http://www.europa. eu.int/comm/eurostat/ [Accessed February 2002]

De Kare-Silver, M (1998) *E-shock: The electronic shopping revolution: strategies for retailers and manufacturers*, Macmillan, Basingstoke

Earl, S E (1986) Staff and peer assessment: measuring an individual's contribution to group performance, *Assessment and Evaluation in Higher Education*, **11** (1), pp 60–69

Eco, U (1994) *Six Walks in the Fictional Woods*, Harvard University Press, Cambridge, Mass.

Edelson, D C, Pea, R D and Gomez, L (1996) Constructivism in the collaboratory, in *Constructivist Learning Environments: Case studies in instructional design*, ed B G Wilson, pp 151–64, Educational Technology, New Jersey

Eduventures.com (2001) *The Education Quarterly Investment Report,Year-end Report 2000: Venture capitalists seek reality, revenues and rational business models* [Online] http://www.eduventures.com [Accessed September 2001]

Ellington, H, Percival, F and Race, P (1993) *Handbook of Educational Technology*, 3rd edn, Kogan Page, London

Evans, P and Wurster,T S (2000) *Blown to Bits: How the new economics of information transforms strategy*, Harvard Business School Press, Boston, Mass.

Ferrarini,T H and Poindexter, S (1999) Web integration in courses: which factors significantly motivate faculty? in *Proceedings of EdMedia 99*, Seattle, USA, June 1999, ed B Collis and R Oliver, pp 512–15, Association for the Advancement of Computing in Education

Foltz, P W, Laham, D and Landauer,T K (1999) Automated essay scoring: applications to educational technology, in *Proceedings Of EdMedia 99*, Seattle, USA, June 1999, ed B Collis and R Oliver, Association for the Advancement of Computing in Education [Online] http://www-psych.nmsu.edu/~pfoltz/reprints/Edmedia99.html [Accessed October 2001]

Gates, W H (1999) *Business @ the Speed of Thought*, Penguin, London

Gokhale, A A (1995) Collaborative learning enhances critical thinking, *Journal of*

Technology Education, **7** (1), pp 22–30 [Online] http://borg.lib.vt.edu/ejournals/JTE/jte-v7n1/gokhale.jte-v7n1.html [Accessed February 2002]

Graf, F and Schnaider, M (1999) Using patterns to efficiently create test for Web-based training, in *Proceedings of Advances in Multimedia and Distance Education Symposium ISIMADE 99*, Baden-Baden, Germany, August 1999, ed M R Syed, O Baiocchi and G E Lasker, International Institute for Advanced Studies in Systems Research and Cybernetics [Online] http://www.igd.fhg.de/~schnaide/papers/ISIMADE99.pdf [Accessed February 2002]

Gunawardena, C N and Zittle, F J (1998) Social presence as a predictor of reported satisfaction within a computer mediated conferencing environment, *American Journal of Distance Education*, **11** (3), pp 8–25

Heywood, J (2000) *Assessment in Higher Education: Student learning, teaching, programmes and institutions*, Jessica Kingsley, London

Hezel, R and Dirr, P (1991) Understanding television-based distance education: identifying barriers to university attendance, *Research in Distance Education*, **3** (1), pp 2–5

Hiltz, S R (1997) Impacts of college-level courses via asynchronous learning networks: some preliminary results, *Journal of Asynchronous Learning Networks (JALN)*, **1** (2) [Online] http://www.aln.org/alnweb/journal/jaln_Vol1issue2.htm [Accessed September 2001]

Hodgkinson, L and Dillon, C (2001) Development and assessment of key skills in the Open University modular environment, in *Proceedings of the 2nd Annual Skills Conference Implementing Skills Development in Higher Education: Reviewing the Territory*, University of Hertfordshire, Hatfield, 11–12 July 2001

Ion, B and O'Donnell, F (1996) Computer aided learning in product design education, presented at the 3rd National Conference on Product Design Education, University of Central Lancashire, 15–16 July 1996

Johnson, R T and Johnson, D W (1986) Action research: cooperative learning in the science classroom, *Science and Children*, **24**, pp 31–32

Kalakota, R and Whinston, A B (1996) *Electronic Commerce: A manager's guide*, Addison-Wesley, Reading, Mass.

Lambert, S and Ropiequet, S (1986) *CD-ROM – the New Papyrus: The current and future state of the art*, Microsoft Press, Redmond, USA

Latchman, H, Kim, J and Tingling, D (1999) BS and MS Online degrees using a lectures on demand approach, *Proceedings of the International Conference on Engineering Education, ICEE 99*, Czech Republic [Online] http://www.fs.vsb.cz/akce/1999/icee99/Proceedings/papers/218/218.htm [Accessed February 2002]

Lave, J and Wenger, E (1991) *Situated Learning: Legitimate peripheral participation*, Cambridge University Press, Cambridge, UK

Lebie, L, Rhoades, A and McGrath, J E (1995) Interaction process in computer mediated and face-to-face groups, *Computer Supported Cooperative Work*, **4** (2/3), pp 127–52

Lessig, L (1999) *Code and Other Laws of Cyberspace*, Basic Books, New York

Litman, J (2000) *Digital Copyright: Protecting intellectual property on the Internet*, Prometheus, New York

Macdonald, J (2001) Exploiting online interactivity to enhance assignment development and feedback in distance education, *Open Learning*, **16** (2), pp 183–89

Mason, R D and Bacsich, P (1998) Embedding computer conferencing into university teaching, *Computers in Education*, **30** (3/4), pp 249–58

Mason, R D and Weller, M J (2000) Factors affecting students' satisfaction on a web course, *Australian Journal of Educational Technology*, **16** (2), pp 173–200 [Online] http://cleo.murdoch.edu.au/ajet/ajet16/mason.html [Accessed November 2001]

Moody, F (1996) *I Sing the Body Electronic*, Coronet, London

Negroponte, N (1996) *Being Digital*, Coronet, London

Noam, E (1995) Electronics and the dim future of university, *Science*, 270, pp 247–49, 13 October [Online] http://www.asis.org/annual-96/noam.html [Accessed November 2001]

Noble, D (1997–2001) *Digital Diploma Mills*: Part I: The automation of higher education (1997), Part II: The coming battle over online instruction (1998), Part III: The bloom is off the rose (1998), Part IV: Rehearsal for the revolution (1999), Part V: Fool's gold (2001) [Online] http://communication.ucsd.edu/dl/ [Accessed February 2002]

Oblinger, D (2001) Will e-business shape the future of open and distance learning? *Open Learning*, **16** (1), pp 9–25

Perry, W (1976) *Open University: A personal account by the first vice-chancellor*, Open University Press, Milton Keynes, UK

Phipps, R and Merisotis, J (1999) *What's the Difference? A review of contemporary research on the effectiveness of distance learning in higher education*, Institute of Higher Education Policy [Online] http://www.ihep.com [Accessed November 2001]

Phipps, R and Merisotis, J (2000) *Quality on the Line: Benchmarks for success in Internet-based distance education*, Institute of Higher Education Policy [Online] http://www.ihep.com [Accessed October 2001]

Plowman, L (1996) What's the story? Narrative and the comprehension of educational interactive media, in *Proceedings of ECCE8: 8th European Conference on Cognitive Ergonomics*, ed T Green, J Cañas and C Warren, pp 167–72

Plowman, L (1997) Getting sidetracked: cognitive overload, narrative and interactive learning environments in *Virtual Learning Environments and the Role of the Teacher, Proceedings of UNESCO/Open University International Colloquium*, Open University, Milton Keynes, UK

Robinson, L A and Weller, M J (2002) Dealing with 12,000 students on an online course, *Education, Communication and Information (ECI)*, **1** (3)

Rogers, E M (1995) *Diffusion of Innovations*, Free Press, New York

Ronen, M and Eliahu, M (2000) Simulation: a bridge between theory and reality: the case of electric circuits, *Journal of Computer Assisted Learning*, **16** (1), pp 14–26

Russell, T L (1999) *The No Significant Difference Phenomenon*, Office of Instructional Telecommunications, North Carolina State University, Chapel Hill, NC [Online] http://teleeducation.nb.ca/nosignificantdifference/ [Accessed September 2001]

Salmon, G (2000) E-Moderating: *The key to teaching and learning online*, Kogan Page, London

Samuelson, P (1996) The copyright grab, *Wired*, **4** (01), January [Online] www.wired.com/wired/archive/4.01/white.paper_pr.html [Accessed December 2001]

Schwartz, E I (1997) *Webonomics: Nine essential principles for growing your business on the world wide web*, Penguin Books, Harmondsworth, UK

Shermis, M D, Mzumara, H R, Olson, J and Harrington, S (2001) Online grading of student essays: PEG goes on the World Wide Web, *Assessment and Evaluation in Higher Education*, **26** (3), pp 247–57

Skillicorn, D B (1996) Using distributed hypermedia for collaborative learning in universities, *Computer Journal*, **6**, pp 471–82

Smith, T L and Ransbottom, S (2000) Digital video in education, in *Distance Learning Technologies: Issues, trends and opportunities*, ed L Lau, pp 124–42, Idea Publishing, Hershey, Pa.

Spender, D (1998) 'Dumbing up or dumbing down?' Key note address at the Communities Networking Conference, Melbourne, 27 February 1998 [Online] http://home.vicnet.net.au/~dukest/dalespen.htm [Accessed October 2001]

Stallman, R (1997) The right to read, *Communications of the ACM*, **40** (2) [Online] http://www.gnu.org/philosophy/right-to-read.htm [Accessed December 2001]

Stamatis, D, Kefalas, P and Kargidis, T (1999) A multi-agent framework to assist networked learning, *Journal of Computer Assisted Learning*, **15** (3), pp 201–10

Treanor, C and Irwin, J P (2001) The world is officially open for business: how MCI WorldCom used the corporate intranet to train a new-era communications company, in *Sustaining Distance Training: Integrating learning technologies into the fabric of the enterprise*, ed Z L Berge, pp 70–84, Jossey-Bass, San Francisco

Tsai, C C, Liu, E Z, Lin, S S J and Yuan, S (2001) Networked peer assessment based on a vee heuristic, *Innovations in Education and Teaching International*, **38** (3), pp 220–29

Ullman, E (1997) *Close to the Machine: Technophilia and its discontents*, City Light, San Francisco

Weller, M J (2000a) Implementing a CMC tutor group for an existing distance education course, *Journal of Computer Assisted Learning*, **16** (3), pp 178–83

Weller, M J (2000b) The use of narrative to provide a cohesive structure for a web based computing course, *Journal of Interactive Media in Education*, August [Online] http://www-jime.open.ac.uk/ [Accessed November 2001]

Young, M F (1993) Instructional design for situated learning, *Educational Technology Research and Development*, **41** (1), pp 43–58

Index

Open and Distance Learning Series

Series Editor: Fred Lockwood